# THE WAY TO LIFE AND IMMORTALITY

First Edition 1914
Reuben Swinburne Clymer

New Edition 2021
Edited by Tarl Warwick

# COPYRIGHT AND DISCLAIMER

# FOREWORD

This present work is a rumination on the capability of immortality (or at least of longevity and health!) from the perspective of Reuben Clymer. The essential message it contains revolves around adherence to an interpretation of mostly Christian lore, and then-modern dietary and lifestyle habits which are herein purported to prevent disease- including diseases now known to be unrelated to the intake of food, breath, etc.

In one very amusing twist, the dietary guide for tuberculosis (consumption) patients is, itself, rather good- eliminating the empty calories of the "bread-and-beer" habits of the lower classes of the early 20th century, suggesting more nourishing food intake, while ignoring germ theory entirely- which makes sense, since Reuben Clymer opposed vaccination and was essentially a more rigorous and thoughtful naturalist, medicinally.

Through adherence to this present interpretation of mostly Biblical dogma, the "Illuminati" spoken of propose to eliminate most human disease, improve breeding, and save mankind, at the ultimate end, from even being mortal.

This edition of "The Way to Life and Immortality" has been carefully edited for format and content. Care has been taken to retain all original intent and meaning.

# THE WAY TO LIFE AND IMMORTALITY

## THE VISION

I lived in an age of strife. All around me were men of ill-temper and ill-will. They fought one against the other, class against class. Even the children took part in the strife and knew no other life than the life of strife, they were ill-shapen and miserable. There was no light shining from their eyes.

The women were in the background, natural prey to the life of strife; for men had no love for each other. When in the midst of clans there was no love the one for the other, and they fought their supposed enemies not because they loved their fellows more, but because they hated their enemies more bitterly.

And out of the midst of the confusion came a Voice to me and bade me look. In the heavens as in a cloud of fire there appeared unto me a vision of two divinely perfect beings. Their bodies were glorious, and as of shining ivory which had life. Out of the eyes looked the Soul of Love. Male and female were they, perfect in soul and in body; for the body showed perfect, and out of the eyes shone the perfect soul.

And as I looked, behold, at their feet appeared children, as perfect as were the other two. It was a vision of Light and Fire, glorious and divine.

But as I gazed, there appeared other full-grown men and women round about them; and in a circle round about them I saw other children and all of them were perfect. There was no mark of disease, no misery, no hate. All was perfection, there was happiness and love, strife had given way. As I gazed upon the glorious vision, a Voice spake unto me:

# THE WAY TO LIFE AND IMMORTALITY

"This is the new heaven and the new earth, the two become one. and I, thy God, shall be with thee." January Eight, 1914.

# THE WAY TO LIFE AND IMMORTALITY

## INTRODUCTORY

The Philosophy, the Religion, the Science, outlined in the present work is that of Manhood- Manhood which is true, strong, virile, but which, strange as it may seem, is in entire harmony with the true conception of Godhood.

In centuries past, up to the present time, mankind has been taught almost universally that, in order to gain the kingdom of heaven, it was necessary for him to deny the body, to crucify the flesh, in fact, practically to destroy the physical. It has been thought that by so doing he would be able to earn the heavenly reward, a place in the heaven of the Great Hereafter. This doctrine was thought to be the means of exalting the soul.

Thus, a premium was placed on souls; but a premium was also placed on weakness of body. Any doctrine, any science, any religion or philosophy, that regards the body as a hindrance, a burden, or even a snare to man, is sure to cause men to neglect physical welfare.

But the new age has set in, a new cycle has begun. Men are no longer taught that the body must be debased and dishonored in order to exalt the soul and to glorify God. To be weak, and delicate in health, to be racked with pain, to be a victim of disease, is no longer thought of as an indication of superior godliness. The teaching of the present age is that man glorifies God by freeing the body of disease and suffering, by making the body strong, by making it as nearly perfect as is possible to make it. The perfecting body and soul, man does, in very truth, glorify God.

But the thinker realize? that teaching of this nature through exaltation of the physical tends toward prolonging life on the earth, and that ultimately and eventually it will lead to physical immortality. He sees that perfection of body, freedom from weakness and disease, perfection in every detail, means an immortal body. The question then arises, Even if it is possible for man so to think and so to live as to build a perfect body, an immortal body, is it really desirable to do so? Considering the conditions under which man lives at the present time, would Immortality on the earth be really advisable?

Were answer given without due consideration, it would naturally be in the negative. Under conditions as they are at the present time, it would not be desirable; for man would not want to live forever where sickness, suffering, sorrow, crime, and vice prevail. But we must remember that as the new age progresses undesirable conditions will pass away.

This is not a modern dream, but was clearly foretold ages ago. The ideal state that results from immortality of body and soul was the theme of the writer of Revelations.

> "And I saw a new heaven and a new earth; for
> the first heaven and the first earth were passed
> away; and there was no more sea.
> And I, John, saw the holy city. New Jerusalem,
> coming down out of heaven, prepared as a bride
> adorned for her husband.
> And I heard a great voice out of heaven crying.
> Behold, the tabernacle of God is with men, and he
> will dwell with them, and they shall be his people,
> and God himself shall be with them, and be their
> God." Rev. 21:1-3.

How many of the vast multitudes who have read these words have had an inkling of an idea of their real significance? These words of the inspired writer mean exactly what they say; yet how many have thought it possible for heaven to pass away? The fact is, little thought has been given to this statement, and men generally have taken it for granted that heaven- that is, the place where souls have gone after death, up to the present time- should continue to exist forever. But John, the greatest of Revelators, clearly states that he saw "the first heaven passed away."

That which is usually called heaven is the state wherein are the souls of those who have passed to the Beyond. It is a state of existence merely, or a plane of being. By Soul Science, it is called the Soul World, or the Soul Realm. It is simply a plane of being to which souls go, and in which they remain temporarily, until they are enabled to return to the earth in order to continue their pilgrimage toward perfection.

To use a homely, but practical, comparison, the Soul World, heaven so-called, is nothing more nor less than a "clearing house." A clearing house is a center in which judgment is passed on checks, drafts, and accounts to determine whether they are valid and worthy of exchange. Somewhat similar to this, all souls, on leaving the body, pass to the soul world, there to await the time when they shall be permitted again to take up the earth pilgrimage in order to free themselves from imperfection. This round of pilgrimages on the earth alternating with temporary sojourns in the soul realm continues until the soul is finally free from all imperfection. When the soul shall have attained Conscious Sonship with God and shall have laid aside all carnality and shall have put on immortality of body and soul, it has no further need of the soul realm.

All souls are given the same opportunity. They are equally endowed by their Creator with the powers and the faculties of the Infinite. Although these powers and faculties are in the beginning potential only, and must be developed in order to be of avail to man in attaining perfection, nevertheless, they are capable of development to such degree that man may indeed attain Godhood and Conscious Immortality in the flesh. Having attained perfection through repeated incarnations, he shall no longer be in need of the soul realm as a "clearing house" through which to pass in order to be tested in regard to the use he has been making of the Infinite possibilities with which he is endowed.

Even though all souls are given the same opportunity and are endowed with divine powers, nevertheless, no Law in heaven or on earth can force men to use their powers in the attainment of perfection. They are given free-will and freedom of choice, and are at liberty to unfold, or to neglect, the Divinity within themselves. He who has persistently neglected the Divine Image in which he is created, he who has persistently and deliberately and willfully lived in ignorance and error and sin through repeated opportunities on the earth plane, will eventually forfeit the right to Individual Perfection and Individual Immortality. In other words, through repeated failure to comply with the necessary conditions of perfection, it is impossible for him to attain perfection because the nucleus of divine powers within, through neglect, will still remain in a state of dormancy. In the event of ultimate failure to comply with the terms of Individual Perfection, the Spark of Divinity within, the soul atom, unawakened to activity, returns in its original condition at the death of the body to the universal storehouse of the Infinite. Yet greatly in the minority are those who neglect or willfully disregard the Divine Law of Life to such degree that Individual Perfection and Individual Godhood are impossible.

Gradually, though to be sure slowly, individual souls are reaching perfection. What then? In so far as the individual soul is concerned, there is no further need of the soul world.

Gradually, though to be sure slowly, all souls that are on the way to perfection will ultimately reach perfection. What then? In so far as these souls are concerned, there is no further need of the soul world.

...That for which there is no further use passes away, Thus, ultimately, the present soul world, "the first heaven," will cease to exist. It is this heaven which John in his prophetic vision declares "was passed away." He foresaw the time when the present heaven to which souls go for a time would no longer he necessary, and, consequently, would no longer exist.

But what in regard to the earth which he saw "was passed away"?

As with the first heaven, so with the first earth. As men become perfect, so will the world and all its conditions become perfect. "The first earth" will have become "a new earth" and heaven and earth shall be one.

But says the critic, Can it be that this earth with its loathsome creeping and crawling things, with its dens of ferocious animals, with its poisonous plants and herbs, with its vipers and insects of deadly bite and sting; this earth with its violent climatic and atmospheric changes, its dread states of turmoil and strife on land and on sea among natural forces and elements, with its horrors and its devastations through fire, water, and wind, with its quakes and its shocks and its volcanic spasms; this earth with its suffering humanity, its injustice, its dens of vice and torture, childhood pinched with cold and starvation, motherhood and womanhood crushed and dishonored and bartered, manhood broken and wrecked through dissipation- can it be that this earth is to become a haven for blissful souls, a heaven, an eternal abiding place for the redeemed and the perfect and for those who have attained the Divine Consciousness?

No, earth as it is, can not be the home of perfect souls. Earth as it is would not be an ideal place for the redeemed of God. Earth as it is would be the veriest hell, a place of torture, for the purified and the cleansed soul.

But earth as it is, is to pass away. This is the vision of John, the Revelator, "the first earth was passed away," and "a new earth" has taken its place.

According as souls on the earth become perfect, in that very degree does the earth as it is, change into the earth as it is to be; in that very degree does "the first earth" pass away and "a new earth" take its place. This is the vision of "a new earth" as the result of perfection of soul. Nor must it be thought of as merely "an interesting coincidence" that perfection of soul and the passing away of the first earth occur simultaneously. It is primarily and fundamentally a matter of cause and effect. Perfection of soul is the cause, "a new earth" is the effect. No, earth cannot be heaven, earth can not be a suitable home for perfect souls, so long as present conditions continue to exist. But equally true is it that present conditions can change for the better only in proportion as souls become perfect. Equally true is it that perfection of soul must become the active cause and the conscious creator of environments suited to the state of perfection.

It is not so difficult to understand that with the progress of soul development economic conditions must improve, and human relationships in every department of life must become more desirable. That perfecting of souls on the earth manifests itself in improvement of humanitarian concerns and in betterment of conditions on the social, industrial, educational, and governmental planes, is a truth already established in the race consciousness.

But that development and perfection of souls on earth has any effect upon the creatures of the earth below man or upon atmospheric and climatic and chemical and other conditions to which man is subject- this thought has meager claim in the race consciousness. This is the truth that awaits the recognition of man. This is a part of the prophetic vision of "a new heaven and a new earth." That mankind has been given "dominion" over creation below him, and that it is his right and his privilege to "subdue the earth" or to exercise his superior creative power in improving the earth- this truth must become clearly outlined in the race consciousness before there can be "a new heaven and a new earth." That the passions and the thoughts and the emotions and the ideals of mankind affect the earth and determine its condition as a dwelling; place for men is a truth of which the Author of these pages is fully convinced, a truth that is to characterize the teachings of the new age. It is a truth that lies at the basis of any rational conception of Immortality.

What is the meaning of the Law expressed by Hermes, the Thrice Wise: "As above, so below"?

As above on the human plane, so below on the physical plane, both vegetable and animal. "As a man thinketh in his heart, so is he." Equally true is it, as a man thinketh in his heart, so are the animal world and the vegetable kingdom around him. For every evil passion, for every evil desire in the heart of man, there is also some evil or unfortunate manifestation in the external world. What man breathes out, animal and vegetable life breathes in and lives upon. Through the exhalations of his thoughts and his passions, man furnishes food and nourishment for the kingdoms below him, both vegetable and animal. The breath of man is loaded with the vitality of his thought creations. If his thoughts are noble, pure and worthy, the emanations exhaled through his breath, being wholesome and vitalizing, feed and support the life of beautiful, valuable creations, as, flowers, herbs, birds, fowls, and animals, of superior order and of beneficent character. If his thoughts and passions are destructive and ignoble, charged with ill-will toward others, the emanations exhaled through his breath are loaded with poisons, and sustain on the planes below him life of an inferior order or even life of a destructive and vicious nature. Thus is it a literal fact "as above, so below." As in the world of human thought and feeling, so is it in the world of manifestation below the human. As is the status of the soul, so is life on the plane below, which feeds upon the exhalations of the bodies and the souls of men.

# THE WAY TO LIFE AND IMMORTALITY

These statements explain how it is a literal fact that man has dominion over the planes below him, that he is in very truth the creator and the nourisher of kingdoms beneath. Neither a myth nor a fancy is it that development of soul on the human plane is both the cause and the creator of "a new heaven and a new earth." In proportion as man's thoughts and passions are exalted and pure, in that proportion are "the first heaven and the first earth passed away," in that proportion is there "a new heaven and a new earth." This fact throws new light on the mission of mankind. Not only creator of his own destiny is he, not only his "brother's keeper" is he, but also in a very remarkable manner is he Lord of creation and Master of both heaven and earth. In a very remarkable manner is he, through thought and desire and emotion and ideal, responsible for external conditions on the earth on which he lives. Through perfection of soul is he responsible for realizing the Divine Purpose, by ushering in "the new heaven and the new earth."

Undesirable conditions on the earth in its physical features as well as in its economic, industrial, and social features are due to the heavy, depressed, poisonous atmosphere emanating from man's thought world. Disasters which result in loss of many lives; devastations and ravages by storm, flood, fire, and wind; violent wreckage of life through pestilence, drought, and famine, and other dire calamities, unaccountable from physical causes merely, are recognized by the Seer as being due to an excessive accumulation of poisonous vibrations from the realm of human thought and feeling. If a fit of anger in the mother is powerful enough to poison the infant at her breast, and cause its death, how much more power for harm and for disaster must there be in the accumulated poison of countless numbers of malicious and perverted lives?

Argument is not needed to prove that mental states of an individual affect his physical condition. The effect of sudden fright, of sad news, of prolonged uncertainty and anxiety, of extreme violence of temper, of intense fear, and of other disturbed mental states, is fully recognized in ordinary experience. The skillful reasoning of a scientist or a psychologist is not needed to convince man of the plausibility of the statement that mental conditions affect the physical being. If mental states are visibly effective in one individual case, how much more effective must be the collective mental states of a multitude of people? It is claimed by scientific investigation that all destructive passions, as, fear, anger, ill-will, malice, hate, melancholy, depression of spirit, form vibrations of heavy, stolid, sluggish character, charged with poisonous elements and explosive substances. As a thunder cloud meeting another storm cloud results in an outburst of forces, liberating the poisonous substances of each, so the collective cross-currents of thought and feeling emanating from many lives result in disasters and calamities, which are too often meekly accepted as "strange but unaccountable ministrations of providence."

On the other hand, if there is such power for harm in destructive and evil mental states, how much power for good must there be in constructive and righteous mental states? Through the collective power of goodness and love and forgiveness and justice emanating from the lives of the many will conditions so change as to make it a desirable habitation for godly souls. The change will be gradual and slow, but eventually and ultimately it will come. The change is now taking place. "The first earth" is even now in process of "passing away." "The new earth" is even now in process of construction. To the Seer of the present age as to the Inspired Revelator of a former age, has been granted the prophetic vision of "the first earth" with its carnality and its distresses and its wreckages "passed away." The Seer of the present day is so fully convinced of the Infinite Power of Goodness operating through Illumined Souls that he clearly sees the earth and its conditions become a fit dwelling place for "the redeemed of the Lord to walk thereon." So fully convinced is he that he is willing to give his life to the promulgation of the truth that leads to such regeneration.

The Philosophy of Analogy reveals a correspondence or a resemblance or a subtle kinship between life in the vegetable and the animal kingdoms and human traits and human characteristics. To illustrate: The serpent has always been considered an emblem of temptation and deception and traitorous tendencies; the dove, an emblem of peace and good-will; the lamb, an emblem of innocence and gentleness; the lily, an emblem of purity and sinlessness; the rose, an emblem of perfection.

Are these emblems merely "a happy coincidence?" Are they nothing more than observations which please and gratify the poetic and aesthetic nature of man? Or is there a fundamental reason, a necessary cause, which makes them not only apt but even vitally and universally significant?

The correctness and the fitness of an analogy is testified to in the fact that it is accepted naturally and spontaneously by mankind in general. To point out an analogy or an emblem is not the result of deep mental study or of close mental reasoning. It is the result of soulful vision, and clear insight info fundamental truth. If the association of qualities indicated by an emblem is true and accurate, the race consciousness accepts it spontaneously and naturally, and forgets to ask why. But the seeker after truth must know why. In time he discovers that there is a fundamental reason for the aptness of all analogy. To illustrate. The snake is an emblem of treachery and deceit, When the heart of man is filled with treacherous and deceitful and traitorous thoughts and desires and motives, the exhalations of his breath are loaded with the particular poison that deceptive thoughts and purposes produce. This outbreathed poison becomes the life and the sustaining force of the animal creation that corresponds to this type of thought. The deadly snake and poisonous viper are sustained and nourished by the destructive exhalations of perverted minds and darkened souls of men. When men cease to have in their hearts the particular passions that the serpent represents and feeds upon, the serpent will cease to exist; or, at least, the serpent will cease to exist as a creature that is loathed and abhorred almost universally by mankind. When man has overcome in his own nature the elements that the serpent represents, he ceases to have a marked abhorrence of the serpent; for there is nothing in his nature that corresponds to it. As an individual he does not furnish it life and nourishment Though it exists, it does not exist as a terror for him. In proportion as the race evolves unto perfection of body, mind, and soul, in that degree will the serpent and deadly vipers and all loathsome creeping, crawling creatures cease to exist as such. If they continue to exist it will be as transfigured creatures, emblems fittingly representative of the graces and the virtues that have supplanted the destructive and the deadly passions that previously existed in the hearts of men.

Thus with all creatures on the animal plane. When the thoughts of men are universally transmuted, when men universally entertain in their hearts only the divine passions of love, forgiveness, good-will, and other holy emotions, instead of the destructive and deadly passions of hate, malice, jealousy, envy, ill-will, and other passions in the category of carnality- then will all undesirable creatures on the animal plane cease to exist. But, just as the evil thoughts of men are the elements whereby undesirable creatures are kept alive, and where-from they live, so do beautiful, creative, constructive thoughts of men give life and nourishment to beautiful creatures on the earth. By universal race consent, the beautiful, delicate, refined flower typifies purity and beauty of character. But the Illumined Soul knows that it typifies purity and beauty of character because it feeds upon and is supported by the emanations of beautiful, refined sorts. The rose has ever been the symbol of the true life, the perfect life; symbol of Illumination of Soul, consequently, symbol of Godhood individualized in man. For this reason has the rose been accepted as the emblem of those who aim at perfection of soul, and for this reason also is the rose a constant incentive to man to strive after the true, the perfect, the beautiful life.

In proportion as the race is redeemed and regenerated in life on all planes, in that proportion will the earth abound in beautiful flowers, luscious fruits, and exquisite flying creatures. As men free their hearts of destructive passions, deadly creatures and poisonous plants will disappear from the earth; and in their stead will come flowers and creatures which are infinitely more beautiful than man in his present state of unfoldment can in his imagination conceive. Thus, in time, the earth will become one beautiful Garden, a very Garden of Eden; and the men and the women thereon will be gods and goddesses, redeemed and perfected souls- perfected so far as our present standards are capable of conceiving, but still evolving new measurements and new standards of perfection, and still striving after and approximating ideals of perfection which surpass the highest measurement of which man is capable at the present time.

Thus is it that man is Lord of all creation. Thus is man to "subdue the earth." Not merely by taming the fierce and the vicious is he to have dominion over the animal kingdom; not merely by destroying the ferocious or by domesticating the wild; not merely by improving species, nor by compelling animal strength to do his will and to bear his burdens; but by living such a holy and sinless life that the emanations of his character act as a redeeming and a regenerating potency in the creation over which he has been made Lord and Master. Not merely by harnessing Nature's forces and bidding them to obey his commands is he to subdue the earth; not merely by mastering the laws to which wind, water, fire, electricity, magnetism, and other natural forces and elements are subject so as to turn their power into channels that serve his purpose; not merely by perfecting flower, plant, and fruit, nor by learning new uses to which they may be put in the economy of human interests- but by living such a holy and sinless life that the vibrations of his soul serve as a harmonizing and redeeming and controlling influence over natural forces and elements, and as a means whereby he is enabled to employ them for constructive purposes, and the radiations for his character give life and nourishment only to that which is beneficial and useful.

The building of "a new heaven and a new earth" is the work of redemption. The work of full and complete redemption does not stop with the salvation of humanity. lo be sure, perfection of soul is the goal and the ideal aimed at. Yet, if man sees no farther than, individual perfection of soul as an ideal, his aim is sadly deficient and largely selfish. Perfection of soul is the ideal aimed at and the standard placed before humanity for the sake of the inevitable results and effects of perfection of soul upon creation as a whole, and upon the earth as a habitation for souls, over which by divine decree man has been made Lord and Master and Redeemer. To aim at individual perfection of soul for its own sake as an individual attainment, though in itself infinitely desirable, falls far short of the heritage granted to man by divine right in that through perfection of soul he is to subdue the earth and to hold dominion over the creatures thereof.

The work of universal redemption and universal regeneration is a slow and a gradual work. But none the less sure is it. Gradually men are beginning to understand the Law that must be obeyed in order to bring about universal redemption. Gradually is there an increase in numbers of those who are striving to live in harmony with the fundamental laws of life. In general, the world is becoming better. And as mankind improves in its life and character, so will the earth become more and more suitable and desirable as the home of Illumined Souls, until finally all things will have become regenerated. Then will there be a new heaven and a new earth. Then the first heaven and the first earth will have passed away.

At the present time there are two planes of existence. There is the earth whereon man rules, largely through evil and destructive methods. There is the soul plane, "the first heaven," wherein imperfect souls abide the opportunity of a return to earth conditions. But, in the coming age, the two shall be one. And God will come out of the first heaven prepared as a bride adorned for her husband. And, behold, the voice of the Great Over-Soul shall say: "God is with men. He dwells with them. They are His people. God Himself is with them and is their God; for He has left the first heaven and has come to earth to be among men. He has become individualized in men. And men have become individualizations of Godhood on the earth."

"This is the new heaven and the new earth" which the Illuminati are teaching men to bring about. They are teaching that strength and perfection for both body and soul is the goal toward which men should strive. They are teaching that the new heaven and the new earth as foretold by the messengers of God can not come until men obey the Divine Law and live a life that is an honor to God, their Creator. They are teaching that to be sickly in body and weak, and to be carnally-minded, is not an honor to God. They advocate that perfection of body and perfection of soul are supplements each of the other, and necessary each to the other.

By no means desirable is it for man to be compelled to live forever on the earth as it is at the present time; but heartily desirable will it be when the world has become regenerated through the regeneration of mankind. Let it be remembered, nevertheless, that Perfection and Regeneration and Salvation and Redemption are ever increasing variables, and that man's conception and standard and measurement of Perfection is an ever increasing variable. The doctrine of full and complete Redemption or Regeneration, the doctrine of Perfection, by no means holds as its ideal a state of bliss that is weak and inert through sheer self-satisfaction or through cessation of growth and activity. Fields of endeavor, realms of achievement, worlds of opportunity for creative power and skill, undreamed of by the most enlivened imagination, await man in the Age of Realization that ushers in "a new heaven and a new earth."

# THE WAY TO LIFE AND IMMORTALITY

May each one who reads and ponders these pages strive to find the Way that leads to Life, Light, Love, and Complete Immortality.

Fraternally,

The Author.
"Beverly."
December Twenty-seven, 1913.

## CHAPTER ONE

### "HEAL THE SICK"

Jesus, whom Soul Scientists and the Illuminati recognize as a Master and as one of the foremost teachers of the Divine Law, gave many admonitions to those who would follow the "Way, the Truth, and the Life"; but no admonition stands out more clearly than the command to heal the sick. In the Gospel of St. Luke are many references to the healing of the sick. The most direct and positive statement given as a command is found in verse nine of chapter ten.

"And heal the sick that are therein, and say unto them, The kingdom of God is come nigh unto you."

Why should the command, "Heal the sick," be accompanied by the statement that those who are healed shall be told that the kingdom of God is come nigh unto them?

The reason for this is to be found in the fact that there is a close connection between health and the kingdom of God, a close connection between disease and the kingdom of error and sin. All illness is due to violation of the laws of health- that is, to some form of sin and error. It may be unconscious sin and error, but it is none the less sin and error. The man or the woman that breaks nature's laws in respect to any one of those things which cause illness, is committing a sin, or violating a law of health. It is to be readily admitted that disease of body and mind is more often due to ignorance than to deliberate wrong doing, ignorance regarding conditions of health, nevertheless, the principle remains true that error in regard to the laws of health results in illness and sufferings, that obedience to the laws of health results in ease and harmony.

# THE WAY TO LIFE AND IMMORTALITY

The fact that there is a vital connection between health and the kingdom of heaven has been overlooked by churches and religious denominations. The church has lost its hold upon humanity largely because it has ceased to make healing of the body a prominent part of its mission. The Temple of Illuminati proposes to reestablish this important feature of religious instruction. One purpose of the Temple of Illuminati is to instruct and to train its members in respect to natural law as it pertains to physical and mental health, strength, and vigor. This it considers to be a necessary feature of the Way to Life and Immortality, Under this instruction and training, the members should not only themselves regain health and strength if lost, but should be qualified to help others in restoring conditions of health, strength, and vitality.

This doctrine, that physical health and vigor are natural manifestations of the kingdom of heaven in human experience, and that disease and suffering are manifestations of the kingdom of error and darkness, is founded upon the Sacred Scriptures. Basis for this doctrine is seen also in the ancient philosophies. It is by no means necessary to use the Bible as authority. However, men generally recognize the teachings of prophets and apostates recorded in the Bible as the foundation upon which all true doctrines rest. There are some, indeed, who consider themselves superior to the instructions of the Scriptures, and who claim no longer to need the Bible; but this very self-deluded superiority shows that they have not yet reached the first steps on the ladder of true Wisdom. All men who have reached Illumination of Soul recognize that the Bible contains the Alpha and Omega of all knowledge, and that therein is clearly indicated the Way to Life and Immortality. Therefore, the teachings of the Scriptures are accepted by the Illuminati as the basis of their instruction; yet it is freely admitted that the sacred writings of other than the so-called Christian religion preserve kindred doctrinists.

Followers of the Illuminati claim that all illness, no matter what its nature, is caused directly through not living in harmony with the Law of God. The Law has two aspects, natural and divine. The Law of God, often designated as "the Law," or "the Divine Law," is both natural and divine, but is often spoken of as one or the other, owing to the prominence of the aspect considered. In general, natural law refers to conditions on the physical and the material plane, and pertains to the physical well-being of man; while divine law, generally considered, refers to conditions which affect the welfare of the soul, and pertains to the spiritual, mental, and divine nature of man. There is, however, no sharp distinction to be made between the two. The welfare of man's spiritual, mental, and divine nature depends upon his physical well-being as a necessary basis. The divine law rests upon the natural law as a foundation. Each is necessary to the other. In fact, it is the same law viewed from different angles.

Thus, let it be clearly understood in the beginning as basic propositions of the Illuminati; first, the state of consciousness designated as "the kingdom of heaven" includes right living (righteousness), or correct habits of life, on the physical plane as well as on the spiritual, or divine, plane of thought; second, any consideration of the Way to Life and Immortality that ignores the physical well-being of man is not only incomplete but even irrational and illogical; third, the command to heal the sick, in face of the vital connection between health and the kingdom of heaven, between illness and the kingdom of sin and error, makes it imperative upon the Temple of Illuminati to give instruction and training concerning the laws of health and concerning a rational basis and method of healing. It is the verdict of physicians that illness is most frequently caused by an erroneous system of living, or by incorrect habits of life; indeed, to give more explicit statement, illness is most frequently caused by an erroneous system of eating.

Time was, when it would have been considered absurd for a teacher, a prophet, a Messiah, to speak of dietetics in connection with Life and Immortality; but that time is past. Now, all wise men, ail truly illuminated ones, know that those things which enter the body as food and drink have much to do with the welfare of mind and soul as well as body. The thoughtful person, the person of keen ambition, no longer considers it absurd or irrational to associate hygienic conditions and scientific dietetics with the Way to Life and Immortality.

Food and drink are to the body what oil is to machinery. A delicate piece of machinery may be thrown out of order and rendered useless by being lubricated with a poor grade of oil. And not until it has been cleaned and recoiled and its equilibrium has been reestablished, can the machine satisfactorily serve the purpose for which it was intended. Likewise, man's organism may be thrown into a state of disorder and inharmony by taking into his system foods or drinks not suited to his needs.

The stomach is the center of motive power for the organism. And, if the part of the organism wherein motive power originates is thrown into a state of inharmony and turmoil, the inharmony is transmitted to the brain through the medium of the sympathetic nerve, and this causes unnatural and morbid thinking. Unnatural and morbid thought conditions, in turn, cause sluggish, ambitionless movements of body. This state of affairs accounts for inefficient workmen and artisans; and, in exaggerated form, it may even account for criminal tendencies and for feeble-mindedness. Furthermore, sluggish, burdened, and depressed condition of physical functions largely explains the prevalent indifference among mankind to the Laws of Life and Immortality.

It is equally important for man to understand natural law as to understand divine law, or spiritual law. Man is well called a prototype of the universe; and, as such, he needs to understand the mechanism of his own structure and the laws of its functions, that he may abide by the dictates of universal law and order. The church of the past has been teaching that souls only are of value, and that the soul can be made immortal, or reach Salvation, regardless of physical conditions. Salvation of soul independent of the body is a doctrine not sanctioned by the Illuminati. Salvation by faith independent of works is not sanctioned by the Illuminati. That faith must be accompanied by works in harmony with the faith professed, that full and perfect salvation of soul is impossible without a corresponding purification of body, are definite tenets of Soul Science and the Illuminati. There is every evidence that the Master Jesus associated salvation of soul with healing of body, and that he identified full and perfect salvation with bodily immortality, and, ultimately, with victory over death.

Possibly the strongest statement that Jesus ever made concerning life and immortality is this:

"Whosoever liveth and believeth in me shall never die. Believest thou this?"

Not only did Jesus teach that man may be healthy and happy, but that, if he is willing to live and to believe in the Christ, he may live forever.

Science is daily proving the possibility of bodily immortality. It is a scientific fact that the physical body of man remakes itself entirely, cell by cell, within a period of nine months. The only reason why the body should see corruption is because man does not live in such a manner that every cell in the body renews itself. Some of the old cells remain. This, in time, causes old age; or, it may even use illness of the physical being, which naturally results in illness or weakness of the mental and the soulual being. Scientific research admits that there is no plausible reason why the body of man should die.

What then should be the remedy for the decrepitude of old age and for other impaired physical conditions? Let the motto of Soul Science and of the Illuminati be the answer to this question:

# THE WAY TO LIFE AND IMMORTALITY

"Our God is the God of life, and not of death."

Let the Law as stated by St. John be the answer to the question: "Whosoever liveth and believeth in the Christ shall not die."

To live in the Christ precedes and accompanies true belief in the Christ. Belief in the Christ is the natural outgrowth of living in him. Jesus nowhere taught that mere belief in the Christ will suffice. He distinctly taught that, in order to attain Christhood, man must live as Jesus lived- that is, in harmony with natural and divine law. Only through right living can man rightly believe. Many claim to have faith in God, who do not live in accordance with the Law of God; but a faith that does not exemplify the Law is, at best, nothing more than a superficial faith. It is a self-deluded belief, which is swept away at the first indication of sorrow or trouble. To weep and to bewail one's fate, to wonder why man should suffer when, as he believes, he trusts in the Lord- this very attitude of mind gives evidence of lack of faith. True faith in God, and living in harmony with natural and divine law are necessary supplements and companions, each of the other.

All science and philosophy support the assertion that it is impossible for a disordered mind resulting from a disordered body to have natural, simple, perfect faith and trust in the Father. It is indeed impossible for the mind to think correctly and to have clear vision when it is depressed and morbid because of physical disorder and sluggishness. On the other hand, when man lives in harmony with natural and divine law, when he observes hygienic conditions and honors the principles of right living on the material plane as well as on the mental and the divine planes, it is natural for him to have a wholesome sincere trust in God, the Father of all. The mind receives none other than cheerful, health-inspiring vibrations from the physical center of life in man; and, it is then easy to believe that there is a God. It is easy to see the beauty in the rose, the harmony in the song of the bird, and in the glorification of God in nature. All is bright, the eye sees the good, and man is become like unto the gods.

That physical health, strength, and vigor characterize him in whom "the kingdom of heaven is nigh at hand," that disease and disorder characterize him in whom the kingdom of sin and error is nigh at hand, are truths which both science and philosophy support. Belief and trust will take tare of themselves when man lives in harmony with both natural and divine law.

The Law of God pertains to life, and has to do with all those things which form a part of daily living. And it is well for man to give careful attention to natural law as well as divine. No one should consider himself too wise, loo far advanced, too refined to acquaint himself with requirements of right living on the physical plane. This includes sleep, work, exercise, breathing, recreation, cleanliness, food, and correct thought habits. It is not uncommon for the student who has reached a certain stage of unfoldment to consider conditions which pertain to physical welfare of inferior significance; and he is inclined to underestimate the importance of the so-called commonplaces of daily life. It should be remembered that the Bible is as much a text-book on hygiene, sanitation, and dietetics as it is a treatise on ethics, salvation, and immortality, and that hygiene, sanitation, and dietetics have a vital connection with salvation and immortality of body and soul. The fact that these relations are a part of the life of man shows that they are important enough to enlist his interest; and, if man desires to attain health and peace, wisdom and immortality, he must, sooner or later, give heed to natural law on the physical plane.

The superficial student may smile at the emphasis placed on the importance of natural law and hygienic conditions; but, if sincere, he need not look far for ample proof of their importance. The fact that obedience to natural law is necessary, and that strict observance of conditions which pertain to sleep, work, exercise, food, breathing, recreation, and cleanliness is a necessary factor of satisfactory living, is not to be overlooked by the sincere seeker after truth.

Furthermore, such items as these are emphasized in this connection because they are necessary features of any legitimate system of healing. Concerning the command, "Heal the sick," it is to be remembered that, as illness is due to violation of natural law in one or more of its aspects, so rational healing must aim at restoring the patient to a normal observance of the conditions violated. That is, if illness is due to a wrong system of eating, or to violation of the laws of sleep and relaxation, or to lack of exercise, or to indifference to internal and external cleanliness, or to an insufficient supply of pure air, or to a combination of such indiscretions, restoration to complete health and harmony of physical functions must include a system of right living in respect to these habits of life.

To live in the Christ, and to believe in Him, insures that man is on the Way to Life and Immortality. To live in the Christ, and to believe, includes obedience to natural law in its different requirements, as, obedience to the laws of health in respect to sleep, nourishment, cleanliness, work, and pure air.

As an illustration of the results of not living in harmony with natural law in its various demands, note that serious, but mysterious trouble called Neurasthenia, or Nerve Starvation. In most cases, there is apparently not a single indication of anything wrong in the physical being, there is no organic trouble, every organ and function seems to be working normally. The physical being, to all appearances, is working naturally and harmoniously.

But how is it with the mind and with the soul of the sufferer? Upon examination of the nervous system as manifest through mind and soul, is found a condition unbelievable to those who have not so suffered. To those who are under the power of the peculiar difficulty called Neurasthenia, there is no sleep; or, if any, it is one horrible dream. There is no peace of mind; for one morbid thought crowds out another, one morbid thought is followed by another. Though the sufferer tries to control the mind, it seems uncontrollable. The eyes cannot be closed; for when they are closed, there appears picture after picture of such things as were never thought of. He may look at the rose, but he sees no beauty in it. He may look at the sun; but, to him, it has no brightness. He may look at the vesture of the fields and the woods. It is useless, for they have for him no charm. He may contemplate life, only to see nothing in it. The Neurasthenic cares for neither love nor beauty, neither life nor death. He knows not why he exists. Speak to him of the soul, he cares not whether he has one. Speak to him of heaven, and he cares not whether there is a heaven or Hades. In fact, for him life is not life, but a continued death.

It was such cases as these of which Jesus said that they had a demon, or even many devils. The mind of such is full of hallucinations. The sufferer knows that these visions, these delusions, are not real; but he is unable to put them aside.

This is but a mild picture of that condition of which millions suffer. It is a condition toward which other millions are rapidly approaching; for it is asserted that the white race is losing its "nerve," and is gradually falling into the neurasthenic state.

What is the cause? Simple or even foolish as it may seem to many, the cause is nothing but starvation of the nerves, due to long-continued breaking of natural law in many of its aspects. In fact, the cause is largely due to a negative state- not doing things that are necessary to normal, natural life, not "living in the Christ." Chief among the causes are violation of simple hygienic conditions, as; insufficient and improper nourishment; hurry and rush in business; insufficiency of sleep, outdoor exercise, and fresh air.

# THE WAY TO LIFE AND IMMORTALITY

It stands to reason that the rational method of treating and of healing a person that has fallen into the clutches of this dread disease must include restoration to normal compliance with the laws of nature previously violated. Of what value would it be to effect an instantaneous miraculous cure, while still permitting the patient to continue in the habits that brought on the difficulty in the first place?

This serves merely as an illustration of the principle that true healing includes instruction in regard to natural as well as divine law; that true healing must touch the life and transform daily habits of living; that true healing teaches one to live, and to believe in, the Christ- to live a life of obedience to natural as well as divine law, and to trust, with sincerity and simplicity of heart, in God, the Father of all. We must live as the Christ lived before we can have undaunted faith in God and in Immortality, before we can ourselves have true health and harmony or help others to attain the same desirable state of being.

Moreover, Soul Science and the Illuminati hold it as a fundamental doctrine, that, if man obeys natural and divine law in their various aspects, and has faith in God, the Father, death of body is not a necessity. Did not Jesus clearly say that the last enemy to be overcome is death? Think ye that Jesus spoke of things that are impossible? Nay, all of this is possible. It is a great and mighty possibility; but, in order to realize this possibility, we must live, and believe in, the Christ. Through the Christ, all things are possible. To obey natural law in its varied conditions; to live in the Christ, and to believe in Him- this is Soul Science, this is the Way to Life and Immortality.

# THE WAY TO LIFE AND IMMORTALITY

## CHAPTER TWO

"And he sent them to preach the kingdom of god^ and to heal the sick"

Those who followed Jesus were given two things to do: to preach the kingdom of God, or to teach the Way to the kingdom of God; and to heal the sick.

It is impossible to separate the one department of work from the other. To attempt to do so, only ends in failure. The established churches have tried to do this for centuries; and it is now admitted even by their own men that results have not been satisfactory.

Why should these two departments of work go hand in hand- "to preach the kingdom of God, and to heal the sick"? Rather, the question would seem more pertinent and rational if it were stated thus: Why should these two departments of work, preaching the kingdom and healing the sick, not go hand in hand? Why should they ever have been separated at all?

Their separation is due to an erroneous interpretation of the kingdom of heaven, an erroneous idea of the relation existing between soul and body, an erroneous idea of salvation and redemption. Naturally, their reunion will be effected through a revival of the true interpretation of the kingdom of God and its relation to man in all departments of his life.

According to the Christie Interpretation, the kingdom of God includes the kingdom of health and right living on the physical plane; salvation of soul cannot be separated from salvation of body; redemption of soul presupposes redemption of body; Life and Immortality, in its full and complete realization, anticipates ultimate victory over death and the grave. When the truth concerning man and his relation to God is fully comprehended, and when man lives the true life, and realizes the ideal relation with God, illness is impossible.

Again and again is it necessary for the Illuminati to be reminded of the saying of John: "Whosoever liveth, and believeth in the Christ shall never die."

Here again are two principles which must not be separated, but which must go hand in hand, living and believing. He who has no faith will not live the life of faith; while he who has faith and lives accordingly will reap the fruits of such living, and the fruits are freedom from disease and death.

The statement that, under any consideration, man shall not see death is, to the sense-bound, sense-loving mind, indeed appalling. Possibly to some, the statement may be even uninviting and gruesome. But, let it be remembered that the promise of never-ending life is only to those who live in the Christ and believe in Him. To those who do not live in the Christ, or live according to His Laws, no such promise is given. Neither are such capable of entertaining a correct conception of the principle of Immortality. Only to the sense-bound, sense-loving nature is the promise of Immortality gruesome and uninviting. To him who has tasted of the sweets of the kingdom, to him who has realized the power and the beauty of life in the Christ, the promise of Immortality is an ideal possible of attainment; but he fully comprehends that its realization comes only through living according to the Laws of the Christ and through faith in the ever-present Christ Principle.

Soul Science and its Christie Interpretation aims at reestablishing the vital and necessary connection between the kingdom of God and the principles of health and healing. It aims at a practical union between preaching the kingdom and healing the sick.

# THE WAY TO LIFE AND IMMORTALITY

It cannot be too strongly impressed upon those who would represent Soul Science and the Illuminati as teachers, that they are to be Healers as well as instructors in the Divine Law. They must be teachers of the truth as interpreted by Soul Science, but they must also become Healers in the true sense of the word, which includes instruction in regard to the method of life that sets man free from disease and suffering.

Among people generally, there is a grievous misconception concerning the healing of the Master Jesus. Many believe that he healed the sick in spite of their sinful life, and that they remained healed in spite of continuing in the old life of sin. This conception is far from the truth. In each instance, Jesus tested the faith of those who came to him for healing; and, when he found it satisfactory, he healed them, but always with the warning that they should sin no more. Well did he understand that health and harmony cannot remain in the body of him who continues in deliberate, persistent sin, especially the sin, or the error, that has been the cause of illness. To heal a man of disease while ignoring the cause, while permitting him to continue in habits that foster disease, is both irrational and unjust. Nor is there the slightest basis for such an interpretation of the cases of healing performed by Jesus and his disciples.

Doubtless, too, a part of the testing of faith was to determine whether the patient understood the law of healing and was willing to free himself from the cause of the difficulty. The faith that does not include a willingness to give up habits of life which cause illness is an irrational as well as an incomplete faith. The faith that expects the man Jesus to effect a cure regardless of cause, the faith that hopes to remain healed regardless of unnatural and abnormal habits of living, is not only crude and deficient, but even savors of sacrilege; for it puts to shame every law of honor and justice. To believe that Jesus instantaneously healed the body of man without pointing out to the sufferer the way by which he might avoid such difficulty in the future, is to make of him a mere wonder-worker and a charlatan.

The work of Soul Science and the Illuminati is to teach mankind the laws of life, to teach men how to live and how to believe, in order that they may become healthy, strong, and efficient. Its mission is an exceedingly practical one. There is the misconception that mystical teaching deals only with the unseen, and, consequently, with theories and with the impractical and the fanciful. This is a grievous mistake. The purpose of Soul Science, in its various departments of instruction, is to make its teachings regarding the Law that leads to Life and Immortality applicable to every-day needs. And what is more needed among mankind than health, strength, and efficiency? Where is there a more exalted and a more practical mission than that of teaching the laws of the kingdom of God together with the laws of health and healing?

This is the New Age, the Age in which man must understand that religion is not merely a system of ideas to be accepted and believed, but that it is the revelation of a mode of life, a life that must be lived daily. Being the revelation of the laws of life, it includes every department of man's nature, and is, therefore, not so much a theory regarding the hereafter as practical instructions which satisfy the daily needs of life here and now.

The end and the aim of life for man is to become like unto the gods. Being endowed with divine qualities and deific attributes and powers, he fulfills his mission in life in proportion as he develops and uses his powers in harmony with universal law and order. When man lives a life that is entirely within the law, entirely natural and normal, he will be free from illness, free from corruption, free from all undesirable things. When man becomes like unto the gods and is fully conscious of his oneness with the Infinite, sin and sickness, death and corruption, no longer form a part of his nature. These statements, to be sure, picture an ideal state; and men generally are by no means capable at the present moment of realizing this state. But to see the ideal and the possibility of its attainment, is necessary as a stimulus to urge one on even to a partial realization.

To live the life of the Christ, does not mean, as formerly held by the churches, merely the redemption of the soul. That idea is forced to give way under the light of understanding that characterizes the present age. Soul Science in its Illuminati teachings maintains that redemption concerns the body of man as well as the soul, that salvation- literally, a making sound, safe, and whole- pertains not only to the soul but to the body also. The more perfect the soul, the more perfect will be its reflection in the body; and, under normal conditions, according to the perfection of the body, so is the perfection of the soul. However, external appearance is not always a reliable index to perfection of body. The physique may be apparently perfect, and yet there may be an internal cancer that is eating away the life of body and soul. To live the life of the Christ refers to true perfection of body and soul. The body that is normal and healthy; the soul that has become enlightened through love, wisdom, and understanding; the soul that is on the way to Illumination and Deific Consciousness; the body that directs its forces into channels of etherealization and immortality- this pictures the true meaning of living in the Christ.

A necessary lesson for the seeking soul to learn is that the body is of prime importance in the work of soul development; that physical perfection helps much, indeed is necessary, in the attainment of soul perfection; that the two- physical culture, aiming at health, strength, and efficiency, and soul culture, aiming at the development of deific powers and deific consciousness- must go hand in hand. If the aspirant is wise he will exercise scrupulous care in regard to the needs of the body in all respects, in order that it may be a stronger help and support to him in his efforts toward advancement of soul.

The student of the kingdom will learn a lesson from the foolish virgins. He will be careful, not only to have a sufficiency of oil for his vessel, but to have oil of superior quality. He will give attention to the amount and to the quality of food and drink taken for nourishment; he will use that only which gives strength and vitality; he will avoid both materials and combinations which interfere with strength and vitality. He must understand that strength, mastery, and supremacy of soul is proportionate to vitality, vigor, and strength of body. He must understand that perfection of body aims at continual, daily transmutation and renewal of cells into cells of a finer and a more spiritual quality, and that this continuous transfiguration of the physical into a higher and a finer type tends constantly toward immortalization of both body and soul.

The church of the past has been active and zealous in its teachings against the use of strong drinks and intoxicants of all kinds. This teaching is to be commended; but Soul Science, in its various branches of instruction, goes farther than this. It recognizes that other drinks than so-called intoxicants are injurious and therefore to be avoided; that inferior quality of foods and indiscreet combinations of food are productive of positive harm to the system, and are therefore to be guarded against. Soul Science makes the claim that poorly selected non-nutritious foods and a wrong combination of foods definitely affect the growth and the purity of man's spiritual being. Many are zealous in their plea for the abolition of spirituous liquors, who are indeed indifferent to the injurious effects of other drinks, and ignorant of the fact that an excess of tea, coffee, and other common beverages acts as poison to the system as truly as does any form of intoxicants.

It is well to understand that "wine is a mocker and that strong drink is raging;" but it is also well to know that other drinks common among men are nerve-wrecking and soul-destroying. It is also well to understand that an excess of certain food elements and a deficiency of other elements cause many ailments to which man is heir, and that, merely by rectifying these excesses and deficiencies, the sufferer may be restored to normal, healthful condition.

In large degree, health is the result of proper nourishment. Certain elements are demanded by the system in order to keep it in perfect condition. In selecting food, not only must the item of nutrition receive attention, but correctness of proportion of necessary elements, and harmonious combination of elements, must be considered. In large degree, disease and suffering are due to improper nourishment, to excesses, to deficiencies, and to unnatural combination of food values.

Thus, the Church of Illumination maintains that its position is sane and logical in claiming that food and drink are legitimate subjects of consideration for those who are truly and deeply interested in the kingdom of heaven and in the healing of the sick. Likewise, it stands on the foundation of reason and practical experience in claiming that full and perfect salvation of soul is impossible in a body that is illy-nourished, racked by starved and sensitive nerves, or poisoned by secretions of useless material.

In face of the command to preach the kingdom of God, and to heal the sick, the advocates of Soul Science consider it their mission to restore proper emphasis upon the intimate and vital relation existing between soul and body. The laws of life as they pertain to hygiene and proper care of the physical being, are as much a feature of the kingdom as are pure thoughts and worthy aspirations. To live and to believe in the Christ, in its full and complete interpretation, includes knowledge of, and obedience to, natural law in its relation to man's physical welfare.

Readers of these lines, and even those who come to the Soul Science Healer for help and advice, may consider that the life advocated by these principles is too ex- acting for them. Possibly after a partial, half-hearted trial, some will return to the old life. In doing so, they take back upon themselves the old weaknesses and the old diseases, perhaps even in exaggerated form. The difficulties and the undesirable effects of the old life are thousand times harder to endure than would be the giving up of a few pet habits which cause the difficulties. Instances of this type must not be thought of as fair representatives of Soul Science healing. They have not given Soul Science principles a fair trial. Nothing but wholehearted loyalty and sympathetic devotion to the principles of life on both the physical and the mental planes can be accepted as a fair and an honest test of Soul Science Healing. In many cases, a satisfactory restoration to health may be effected by competent Soul Science Healers in a very short period of time; but the one who is healed must remember to "go his way and sin no more," lest a worse evil befall him.

However, it must not be thought that the new life, the life advocated by Illuminati principles, is painfully exacting and difficult to follow. Rather, is the reverse true. The results are so beneficial that it becomes a delight to perfect oneself in the practice of its principles. Often a few simple changes in the daily habits of life will be all that is necessary to effect a satisfactory restoration to normal health and strength. A few non-essential items, which would never have been indulged in were it not for erroneous teachings, may need to be rectified or dropped out of the life. The cross that Soul Science principles imposes is not hard to bear; for it denies man none of the things that give true pleasure, none of the things that prove of benefit to him. It prohibits only those things which give slight, temporary, short-lived pleasure followed by greater pain.

The standard of the Soul Science Healer is: "Whosoever liveth and believeth in the Christ shall not die."

He teaches a system of normal, natural living, as regards habits which affect physical health and spiritual vigor. He teaches a philosophy that promotes right thought and right action in the individual life. His purpose is to touch the mainspring of thought and motive, and to lift the standard of thought to the plane of Life and Immortality, away from the plane of disease and death. He must instill into his patient the conviction that man must live right if he would be free from disease and suffering and death. When the seeker understands these things, the Healer can effectively say unto him: "Thy sins be forgiven thee, go thy way and sin no more." And thus shall it be; for marvelous power is entrusted to the true Soul Science Healer.

The Soul Science Healer is permeated, charged, with faith in God; for he is convinced that our God is a God of life and not of death. He is convinced that mortality shall put on immortality. Is there a thought in any language of deeper significance than this? The mission of Soul Science is to help man put on immortality; for it teaches him to think correctly and to live correctly. When man persists in correct habits of thought and in correct habits of life, he will find that mortality is passing into immortality, that the bodily cells are daily being transmuted into cells of a finer quality. He who liveth and thinketh in the Christ will gradually become more and more like Him. This is the promise that the Father, Giver of Life, gave to mankind not only through Jesus, who became the Christ by following this doctrine, but through evil the great Masters and Initiates of the past.

It is to be admitted that many men who have understood the Law and have lived in harmony with it to the best of their ability, have tasted of death and passed on to their fathers. This fact is explained in the power of the race belief in the necessity of death. The race, as a whole, has taken it for granted that death is a necessity, that immortality is an impossibility. But this belief is rapidly giving way to the belief that physical death is not a necessity. Consequently, men are seeking the way by which man may avoid death. This is the mission of Soul Science and Illuminati instructions- to break the shackles of race belief in death, and to teach mankind the Way, the Truth, and the Life that leads to Immortality.

# THE WAY TO LIFE AND IMMORTALITY

The question is asked, What becomes of the millions who have lived in the past and who have tasted of death of the body.

Many of these are now on the earth. Others will again return to earth. Ultimately, all, with the exception of those who destroy their own individuality through deliberate wrong doing, will have repeated the earth pilgrimage until they have attained perfection. When that time shall have come, sons and daughters will be born to parents in perfection; and the millennium will have dawned, not through faith alone, but through faith combined with, and exemplified through, works.

Soul Science and its Illuminati teachings will cause its watchword, "God is the God of life and not of death," to resound through the whole world; and those who suffer in body and in soul will seek its temples for instruction and healing.

Were it not true that the body of man is of value, and needs to be exalted and honored with immortality, God, the Father, and His messengers would never have called it, the Temple of the Soul, or the Temple of the living God. That the soul may be perfect, the temple must be made pure and holy, and must be honored with perfection. This is attained by having confidence in the promises given by God to man and by living in harmony with the laws of perfection. He who so believes and who so lives, is daily attaining perfection. It cannot be otherwise; for he is meeting the necessary conditions of perfection.

Our God, who is "the God of life and not of death," says that man shall not see death if he lives and believes in the Christ. But He also says with equal emphasis, "The soul that sinneth it shall die." Equally true is it that the body that sinneth, and lives not in harmony with natural and divine law as exemplified by the Christ, shall also die. This is not because God desires it so, or arbitrarily wills it so, but because violation of law is its own penalty. He who violates the law of harmony suffers the inconvenience of inharmony. He who violates the law of order must suffer the natural consequences of disorder. He who violates the laws of health must endure illness and disease. He who lives in harmony with universal law and order, reaps the benefits of peace and harmony. He who pays the price of life and immortality reaps the blessings of life and immortality. He who lives and believes in the Christ passes from mortality to immortality. He who obeys natural and divine law, proves that there is no eternal death.

Gradually, belief in the necessity of death and in the impossibility of immortality shall give way to the conviction that our God is the God of life and not of death, and that he who liveth and believeth in the Christ shall not die. Believest thou this?

## CHAPTER THREE

## BELIEF IN DEATH BRINGS DEATH. BELIEF IN LIFE BRINGS MORE OF LIFE

Up to the present time, mankind generally, including the Church Fathers, has believed in a God of death. It has been the prevalent belief that man must die. Furthermore, it has been considered that sickness and suffering are the natural states of man; thus, the entire race has been inoculated with belief in disease and death. It seems strange that this should be the case; for the Master Jesus clearly taught that whosoever believes and lives in the Christ shall not die.

This doctrine of the Master Jesus positively declares that the state of illness and death has no part in the nature of man, and therefore should not have a place in his belief. And yet man is just awakening to the fact that somewhere he has been making a mistake all these years. He is awakening to the fact, that, instead of having faith in Life and Immortality, and in a God of life, he has been holding to the race belief in disease and suffering, in a God of death, and in mortality instead of Immortality.

This race belief, the continual belief in disease and death as man's inheritance, has acted as a slow, death-dealing poison, as a virus, which has inoculated his system and has brought upon him these very conditions; and, thus, he has been burdened with disease, and the end thereof has been death.

But the two thousand years of the old cycle are ended and the new cycle is ushered in. With the ushering in of the new cycle, from the very beginning, the Illuminati have stood for a God of life as opposed to a God of death, for the changing- of mortality into immortality, and for the doctrine that man is not "a worm of the dust," but "a child of the King," a child of God, the Father, and that his rightful inheritance is Immortality and Godhood. The Illuminati are doing all in their power to break away the chains of bondage to the belief that disease and death are man's inevitable heritage. They stand firmly and openly for the conviction that man's destiny is to become like God, the Father, his Creator; that his mission is to express the divine character and attributes, and to exemplify his divine possibilities.

Thus, the Temple of Illuminati and its doctrines of Soul Science says to its disciples:

Put away from you the old idea that man must forever suffer and be in sorrow. Put away from you the idea of death. Establish in your hearts an active faith in the possibility of continued good health and of immortality. Break the fetters that bind you to the old race belief in the necessity of disease and death. Live right, live simply and normally, and in accordance with natural and divine law; and you will free yourself from disease and, ultimately, from the old enemy, death. This is the doctrine of the Illuminati, the doctrine of the coming Bride of the Christ.

Not only is it necessary to put aside forever the race belief in the necessity of disease, sorrow, and death, but it is also necessary to have an active, abiding faith in the power and faithfulness of the All Father, and in His promises that man may have health and happiness and may become as one of the Gods. Furthermore, it is absolutely necessary for him to live according to this faith and to cultivate habits of life which exemplify this faith. The habits of life that exemplify a true faith in the All Father include conditions which affect man's physical welfare, such as, sleep, rest, food, exercise, and work.

Worry, haste, improper eating and drinking are items that must be rectified. The one who seeks to personify Illuminati principles must honor physical exercise, rest and recreation, and the natural elements- air, light, and sunshine. He must so arrange his interests as to apportion his time between active work, rest and relaxation, exercise and innocent pleasures, including those things which, under normal conditions, bring happiness to man.

Under the item of eating, he must guard against those elements which are not conducive to his welfare in every respect. Perhaps there is no habit more detrimental to general health than the use of sweets and starches in abundance and to the exclusion of the necessary nerve-and-vitality-building foods. For, if we use an excess of sweets and starchy elements, naturally we cannot take as much of the vital foods as the system demands; and the result is disease, old age, and death. In regard to drinks, man must learn to avoid those which are stimulating, and must indulge more freely in those which are eliminating in character. When these suggestions in regard to food and drink are observed, balance, or harmonious adjustment of forces, results, which is conducive to health, efficiency, youth, and long life.

Under present economic conditions, with the exception of the hard working manual laborer, man should free himself almost entirely from the use of starchy foods and the use of white, denatured bread. White, denatured flour in all its products should have no part in his dietary. It is such foods as these, including refined sugars, which rob the system of the natural clime necessary to its welfare, and which produce the abnormal craving for tea, coffee, and strong drink. Because of abnormal craving, man thinks that he needs these products and therefore indulges in them freely, only to find that they are superficial and temporary in their effects, and not of vital, permanent value to the organism. Cut, when the proper foods are taken into the system, this abnormal craving gradually diminishes, and an actual building up of the system results; and the organism becomes free from those serums which cause illness, old age, and death.

The Soul Scientist treats not only the soul but the physical man as well; for he knows that the Immortal Soul must have its foundation in a normal, healthy body. Otherwise, the soul can not develop permanency of individual existence. The Illuminati principles, through Soul Science, deals with the whole being. In this, they follow the command of the Master Jesus and all other true Masters and Initiates in their emphasis on Life and Immortality, and an active faith.

The faith advocated by Soul Science is not a fanatical faith, but a faith that is founded on reason and on the truth. It is practical results which prove the truth or the falsity, the benefit or the disadvantage, of a system of belief or a doctrine. It has been brought to a satisfactory test time and again that, when man obeys the principles of Soul Science and gives them a thorough, faithful trial, in every instance health, peace, and efficiency have been the fruits. In face of these results, followers of Soul Science instructions are becoming ever more zealous in the propagation of their principles. They are daily more fully convinced that theirs is a normal, rational faith, based on the Christie Interpretation of Truth.

The old doctrine has been that the chief aim and end of life is "'to glorify God, and to enjoy oneself forever." When one seriously considers the meaning of the expression, "to glorify God," one is willing to admit that it is all-inclusive in its scope, and that it may well be thought of as "the chief end and aim of life." But, alas, how few give these words a single serious thought!

How can man better glorify God than by becoming like Him? How better, than by living such a normal, happy life as to free himself from the conditions of ill-health, suffering, and sorrow? How better, than to say: Here am I, my body is perfect, and functions as freely and as regularly as the universe, part of which I am. Here I stand, not only with a perfect body, but with a soul that is also perfect in its activities. My body is like the universe in its obedience to law and order. My soul is like the

Father who rules the universe. Though but a small being, a little universe, a Microcosm, my perfection is fashioned after the great universe, the Macrocosm; and my Soul daily inhales the perfection of the Father who rules the Universe. I am daily obeying the command, "Be ye therefore perfect even as your Father in heaven is perfect."

However extravagant these words may seem to the sense-bound, sense-loving mind, there is nothing of sacrilege or of blasphemy in them. They merely express obedience to the standards of the Master Jesus after finding the Perfect Soul, the Christ, within himself. When properly understood, they express humility, the deepest man can know; self-renunciation, the most complete; sincerity and simplicity of trust in God, the Father, rather than in the self, the most profound possible to man.

In reaching this stage of perfection, he still remains man; and it is then that he can enjoy himself forever. Again, in reaching this stage of perfection, man is not required to give up a single thing that brings true enjoyment or true happiness. He gives up only those things which bring a temporary enjoyment, but which, like a thief in the night, rob him of tenfold more than they bring. No seeker need think that he is called upon to give up the pleasures that belong to the normal human being. Such is not the case. Only those things which bring pain or sorrow to the one indulging in them or to another are forbidden man. It is well to accept the principle that the chief end of life is to glorify God and to enjoy oneself forever; but it must be remembered that enjoyment can be true enjoyment only when it is at the expense neither of the self nor of any other human being.

Under the old race belief that man must be sick, that he must suffer, and that death is the end of all, there could be no sure and lasting enjoyment; for in the midst of pleasure comes the thought of illness and death. But, under the new dispensation, all this passes away; and man knows that he need not "surely die," but that he may "surely live," if he is only willing to live the life of the Christ-life, as Soul Science and the Illuminati teach it, a natural, normal, and blessed life.

But this is not all. In obtaining freedom for the physical being, the Temple, there is also obtained something even greater- that is, nothing less than Illumination of Soul. It is herein that the Soul Scientist finds his strongest basis for belief in the Fatherhood of God and in the Immortality of the Soul; for, when he obeys the natural and divine laws, when he obtains freedom for the body, he also obtains liberty for the soul Through continued living the life of the Christ, there takes place gradually the new birth of the soul. Then the soul comes to see and to know those things which the mere physical man can never know. Consequently, man becomes, in truth, like one of the Gods; for he has freedom for the physical being, and liberty and clear vision for the Inner Being, the Immortal Soul.

It is the soul in man that is striving for liberty, and for enlightenment. The soul in man has been striving for its higher freedom, lo, these many years; but man has been held down by the race belief. And a few, perhaps only one in a million, ever comes to think and to act in advance of the age in which he lives. The general race belief has been holding mankind almost universally in bondage, and causes men individually to shrink in horror from thinking and believing that which is not accepted by the many. But the soul is gaining superiority over its environments. The general belief in disease and death is broken. The new cycle and the new dispensation have brought in a new era, a time in which man shall no longer fear to think, no longer fear to cast off the shackles that have bound him. The new era is helping man to know the truth and to overcome "the last enemy, death."

The Illuminati, through the medium of Soul Science, have been laboring in the field these many years, teaching that the soul of man is immortal, that the body of man may be brought to a state of freedom from corruption, that all men may draw upon the universal, spirit of God as freely and as fully as they choose, and thus have life ever more abundantly. While on earth, the Master Jesus taught mankind "the Way, the Truth, and the Life." But that few understood what he meant by "the Way, the Truth, and the Life," is seen in the fact that on all sides are misery and sorrow, disease and corruption; and vast multitudes believe that only in death are peace and happiness to be found. The multitudes have forgotten that Jesus taught that the truth would bring life, and life more abundantly; that his teachings would be as bread come down from heaven; that he who partakes freely of the teachings should have life and not death. Mankind has been blind these many centuries, and has not been able to believe that life and not death, enjoyment and not sorrow, should be the common lot of man.

This truth, that the end and the aim of life is to glorify God and to exemplify the principle that our God is a God of life and not of death, the Illuminati through its Soul Science have been teaching- truth pure and clear as it comes from the very fountain of life. This truth is not given in symbolism and in obscure phraseology so that only the few can understand, but in clear language and in ringing tones, so that all may comprehend, so that all who will may live the life and reap the fruits of such living.

The Illuminati and the disciples of Soul Science say unto all:

Learn the truth, live according to the truth. Believe actively that life in the Christ is good; that man is not born to suffering and disease; that man need not always be a creature of pain and misery if he is willing to live in harmony with natural and divine law. Let each one live in harmony with the truth that man is made in the image of the Creator, God. Put away from you now and forever the thought that you must suffer and "surely die." Put in its place the conviction that you are a child of God, that the Father has given you all power; that sickness and death are not for

you, but that more and continually more and more of life are
yours, and that the more abundant life ends in Immortality. Free
yourself from the race belief in the necessity of sin, disease, and
death; for this very belief attracts the object of its faith and tends
toward the conditions that it represents. Know that God is good,
that in the Universal Storehouse of God there is life- life free and
abundant- and that you may draw therefrom according to your
need. Know that, for drawing upon the vibrations of life from the
Infinite Storehouse, the only requisite is faith in God and in
yourself, faith that enables you to live the normal, natural life- life
free from destructive conditions, life that accepts nothing, neither
thought nor desire, neither food nor drink, which may in any way
prove detrimental to continued life.

The Soul Science Healer teaches his people such truths as
these. He teaches them how to live; how to draw upon the Infinite
Supply of Life, Love, and Wisdom; how to bring their being into
harmony with the Universal Law, and to free themselves from
disease, suffering, and other undesirable conditions. He teaches
faith, as the beginning of the new life; but he teaches works as a
necessary part of an active faith. He teaches man to think right, to
believe right, and to entertain right desires; and, as a consequence
of constructive thought, correct belief, and worthy desires, his life
will be in harmony with the Universal Law, and, eventually,
mortality will put on Immortality.

## CHAPTER FOUR

## THE LIFE WITHOUT DEATH IS GOD'S PLAN

In allowing the divine spark to leave the heavenly spheres and to incarnate in a physical, or earthly, body on this plane, it was God's plan that, first, through incarnation, the divine spark should become a personality, separate from God, the All Creator, and, that, second, the personality, through development, should become an individuality, or conscious self-existent being. Through the attainment of personality and of individuality, the soul spark is destined to pass through the knowledge of good and evil, pain and sorrow; but it is not the divine plan for it to stop with this. According to the divine purpose, the soul is to go onward and upward until it reaches the Sublime Realization, that which, the Illuminati in their Soul Science call Illumination of Soul.

Between the man who is simply a personality and the man who has reached individuality, there is a mighty gulf. The one is of the flesh and lives in the flesh. He may believe in God; but he does not know God. He is a carnal being with carnal desires, and, at best, is little more than "a worm of the dust." He has little comprehension of the divine possibilities latent in his own being. He has but meager aspirations for higher and better achievements. Far different is the man who has attained individuality. He has awakened to the real meaning of the principles of Jesus and other great Masters. He is filled with a burning desire to live in harmony with these principles, and to test the highest standards of life. His ambition runs in channels of true development. He aspires after a full and complete consciousness of his own Oneness with the Infinite. Through lofty and worthy aspirations, and through a life of self-sacrifice and of usefulness to others, he arouses the divine spark, the soul, within his own being, into a state of consciousness and of dynamic activity. Thus, the divine spark of a soul develops gradually into the Christ, or the Christos, the Son of God.

# THE WAY TO LIFE AND IMMORTALITY

Moreover, in the full realization of the Christos, the individual will comprehend the significance of the promise that the last enemy, death, is to be overcome. He will understand that this promise may actually be fulfilled; furthermore, he will understand how the promise is to be fulfilled. He will perceive that it is possible for the time to come when man shall no more be sick, and shall no more know death. In the full realization of the Christos, he becomes truly conscious of his Sonship with the Father; the Dove of Peace descends upon him, and, in unmistakable tones, says: "This is my beloved Son in whom I am well pleased."

This is the Sublime Realization, It is the end and the aim of man's life on earth. Moreover, cycle upon cycle shall pass, man shall return to the earth plane again and again until he has received this Sublime Realization, this Divine Illumination. It is the purpose and the plan of God, the Heavenly Father, the Infinite Creator, for man to attain this realization. However, in infinite wisdom, He has endowed man with free-will and with right of choice; and he is therefore free to accept or to reject "the Way, the Truth, and the Life" that leads to this exalted Consciousness.

Two possibilities are placed before man, subject to his freedom of choice. The one opens to him the opportunity of unfolding his divine nature and of developing his deific attributes, thus exemplifying the fact of his being made in the divine image. This path leads to the Sublime Realization of Sonship with God, the Father. It is the path of self-crucifixion and of Christ Exaltation. It is marked by purity of thought and purpose, and by a continual surrender of the carnal nature to the Christ Ideal, a continual transmutation of the baser metals of the lower personality into the pure gold of spirituality. It is development of soul, which culminates in an Immortal Individuality. Its chief marks are goodness and service to others. But, if man does not, of his own free choice, travel this path and meet the full requirement of its conditions, he pays the penalty of retrogression; and the divine spark of a soul smolders under the ashes of selfishness and carnality. He may repeat the earth life time and time again; but, if he persists in deliberate sin and wrong doing, he will eventually be thrown back to the elements whence he came. The divine spark, not having attained individuality, returns to the Father, losing its identity in the storehouse of universal essences. The body returns to mother earth whence its elements came. Cycle upon cycle shall pass, man shall return again and again, until he has either attained the Sublime Realization or has been thrown back to the original elements.

The end and the goal of life is attained in the Sublime Realization of Oneness with God. This, both in the process of attainment and in the realization, is a life of service to humanity. It is a life of faith, a life attended by the works of faith.

The ordinary man does not really believe the promises of God. He thinks that he believes; but the conditions of his life prove that his faith is not true faith. For, if he actually believes in the promises, he will live according to them, and will do the works of faith in a life of goodness and helpful service to others. And, when he faithfully lives in harmony with the promises of a true faith, he will not be continually harassed by illness, suffering, and torment. The suffering of the multitudes round about us indicates that men generally have not a true faith in God or in the promises of God.

The first step to be taken in the search for freedom- freedom from all undesirable conditions- is a step of faith. It is for man to muster faith in God and in His promises. It matters not whether he learns of these promises through the Sacred Scriptures or through the old philosophies- it is for him to muster indomitable courage and an invincible faith in the verity of the promises of God to man. He must put his faith into practice and live daily the deeds and the aspirations of faith. As he lives the life of faith, he will reap the rewards of such a life. The results include a greater knowledge; and, as knowledge increases, faith increases and intensifies, enabling him to live a still more nearly perfect life. Man must use the one talent that he has; and, as he does so, other talents will be given him, until finally all the talents will be his. Such is the promise.

In the hearts of all men there is a divine impulse. The multitudes scarcely know what this impulse is; but the fact remains that there is such an impulse within them, there is an "inner urge" for something which they have not. This urge is constant, day and night, year in and year out. This is the divine impulse given to man, or placed in the heart of man by his God, urging him to seek, and to put forth effort to attain, the Sublime Realization of God. If man begins to listen to this urge within and to heed its intimations, it will lead him ever upward and onward. As he follows one good impulse, another will take its place. Thus, step by step, he is led to the Divine Realization. In proportion as he realizes the Sublime Consciousness, in that proportion will he experience health and peace and happiness. And, as he substitutes in place of the race belief in the necessity of death the conviction that our God is a God of life and not of death, so will he eventually overcome the last great enemy, death.

All philosophies have taught the deathless life, and broadly hinted at the time coming when man should not die, when he should reach perfection of both body and soul here on the earth plane. However, it remained for Jesus to demonstrate to mankind the possibility of perfecting the physical being, perfecting it to such degree that it might even be taken up again after being laid down in the throes of death.

And, just as Jesus lived the life that led him to the Sublime Realization, to the deathless life, so did he give man the promise and the instructions that should lead him also to the deathless life. But man has not believed deeply enough to obtain the promised deathless life, the life that should reach the ultimate. Of the teachings, which, according to his claim, were given him from the Father for mankind, this is a clear statement: "Whosoever shall eat of the bread that I give, shall have eternal life." The bread to which he refers is wisdom, and true understanding of the laws of life. The man who lives according to the Christie laws shall have life unto eternity- Moreover, the life shall be one of peace, of happiness, and of contentment.

It is these sublime teachings- the Christie Interpretation of "the bread of life"- teachings covered over by centuries of creedism, which the Temple of Illuminati places before all peoples. Whosoever is willing to live according to these teachings shall find health and freedom from the miseries that are the common lot of mankind at the present time. This is the divine purpose, the divine plan, for man- to attain the Sublime Realization of life without death. To support this divine purpose, and to reestablish faith in this divine plan, is the mission of Soul Science and Illuminati instructions.

The doctrine of life without death is based on the Christic Interpretation of the Divine Law, on the Sacred Scriptures, and on the ancient philosophies as understood by all great Masters and true Initiates. That the ultimate of man's destiny is life eternal and consciousness of immortality, has ever been the standard of all true Initiation. That such victory over death as our Master Jesus demonstrated is for all who will meet the requirements of the Divine Law as he met them in actual experience, is the honest conviction of the advocates of Soul Science and Illuminati principles.

But let no one think that, by any miraculous display, man may jump into such power at one bound. Such power is the culmination of soul development extending through repeated earth pilgrimages; rather, it is the culmination of a development of both body and soul through repeated incarnations in harmony with both natural and divine law. That there is a science of development for both body and soul, a science that explains laws and methods, and points out "the Way, the Truth, and the Life" underlying such development, is the conviction of the Illuminati. To teach mankind these laws of development on both the physical and the spiritual plane, is the purpose of Soul Science. In this sense, Soul Science is the Way to Immortality.

First of all, must be broken the fetters of a longstanding belief in the necessity of sin, disease, and death; and there must be substituted in the hearts of men the conviction that sin, disease, and death are not according to the divine purpose for man, but that, being created in the image of God, man is endowed with divine attributes and divine powers, which, when developed and used, will enable him, ultimately, to overcome even the grim monster death.

Advancement in any line demands a beginning. With many into whose hands these pages fall, a beginning has already been made. The fact that one ponders these words with carefulness and with interest is proof of some sort of a beginning. Interest in this trend of thought, and a desire to search after truth, indicate that a necessary step has been taken. It is only required for the earnest seeker after truth to persist in overcoming carnality and the supremacy of the lower nature. He must persist in freeing himself from carnal desires and from the tendency to indulge in negative destructive thought habits; for carnal desires and negative thought conditions tend toward death. With many who read these words, a beginning in the new life has been made in a previous incarnation and perhaps, even many steps may have been taken on the path of attainment; yet it will still seem that new beginnings are often required before they reach the goal of their aspirations. To make a new start under new conditions, each time adds zest, and marks a step of progress in the path of advancement.

Man may be thoroughly convinced that life according to the Divine Plan is the only true and satisfactory life; yet it seems easier to follow the dictates and the intimations of the carnal self, while persistent effort is required in living the Ideal established by the Divine Plan. Consequently, the majority of mankind are following the desires of the personality, and are living in harmony with them. This path leads ever toward disease and death.

But, gradually, soon, even in this age, things are to change. Great changes have already taken place. Man is beginning to think, he is searching for the cause of conditions. He is investigating the relation between cause and effect. He questions, why such misery and such suffering. He beholds the character of life led by mankind generally, he associates the cause with the life, and knows that something is lacking. Gradually, he comes to the conclusion, that, having tried the old way, lo, these many centuries, he will now try the new; for the new can not be worse than the old. As he begins the new life and lives the life of faith attended by works corresponding to the faith, results are gratifying, even more gratifying than he had anticipated or had even thought possible. Thus, not the one, nor yet the few, but even the many, are being awakened to the spirit of the new age. The past race belief in bondage and death is being transplanted by the new race belief in freedom and life.

It is not difficult to determine the reason for conditions when one remembers the law of correspondence. There is a law of correspondence between all things, between that which is above and that which is below, between the universe and God, between the universe and man, and even between man and his God and Creator. Man partakes of both heaven and earth. The body is of the earth, earthy. The soul is of the heavens, heavenly. Condition depends on which power is in the ascendancy. If the body and its desires are in the ascendancy, the conditions of man's life tend toward disease and death. If the soul is in the ascendancy, and the body is a faithful servant to the soul, then man's life and character exemplify satisfactory correspondence with God and the universe, and manifest the fact of his being created in the divine image.

# THE WAY TO LIFE AND IMMORTALITY

With the exception of the Illuminated ones, to the man of the present age, the soul is merely a weird something to believe in, something of which he has no certain knowledge, while the body is tangible and visible, something that feels pleasure and pain. Consequently, the body is a reality, and the soul is at best but a fanciful theory. Being to him a reality, the body has a right to claim supreme attention. And it is in every way to his interest to cater to the desires and the appetites of the body, notwithstanding it is these very desires and appetites which, when indulged in to excess or contrary to the wise guidance of the soul, lead to disease and death. Until the desires of the body have been made subservient to the wisdom of the soul they lead downwards. For centuries, mankind has listened to the desires of the body regardless of the higher interests of the soul. Thus, the body, being of the earth, earthy, tending toward disease and suffering and death, has been holding supremacy in the life of mankind.

The desires of the soul are different both in immediate effects and in permanent results. The soul, being of God, in its desires and its inclinations, reaches upward. But, being unseen and merely felt, man has put aside the impulses and the intuitions of the soul, he has covered them up; and the result is that the soul of man has been sleeping the sleep of dormancy and inactivity.

When the voice of the soul, the divine urge, is heard and obeyed, then, step by step, the soul leads itself and the body upward until eventually the Sublime Realization of life without death is reached. Thus, man frees himself not only from disease and death, but also from all other undesirable things. In addition, besides thus freeing itself, the soul has come into harmony with the Father, it has become Illuminated, a living Son of God, one in whom the Father is well pleased.

This type of life, in which the soul holds the supremacy over the body, is the life the Master Jesus lived. He had faith in the teachings of the Masters of old. And, as he lived in harmony with

the laws of their teachings, he gradually grew into the Divine
Realization, until, at last, he had so purified and refined the body
that it was free from sickness and from misery, and was qualified
to manifest ultimate victory over death and to come into the Glory
of God while in the flesh.

According to the divine promise, all men can, if they will,
live the life that Jesus lived; and, through faithful, persistent
obedience to the Law and through service to humanity, it is
possible for all men to reach the Divine Realization and 'to come
into the Glory of God while here on the earth.

It must not be thought that such a life as Jesus lived in
order to attain victory over death and the grave is not a real or a
practical life. Directly the contrary is true. The true man is neither
a parasite nor an unprofitable member of society. The true man
lives a life of service to others. He engages in business, and fulfills
the duties that devolve on all men. He is faithful to the duties of
home life and neighborhood interests, and is responsive to the
demands of society at large. Nor must it be thought that he who
desires to realize the power of the Christ over death and the grave
is to deny himself all pleasures and all recreation and all delights.
Directly the contrary is true. He is entitled to innocent and
harmless pleasures and recreations and to all those things in which
the healthy, normal human being delights. The only check on
pleasure of any description is the provision that it shall be free
from harm to himself and to others.

Man is by nature a social being. Of all things created, he is
the only one to which is given the smile and the laugh. This in
itself indicates that the social instinct and the gift of smile and
laughter were given him for a purpose. The more he encourages
the wholesome spirit of merriment and amiability, the better it is
for himself and for those with whom he comes in contact. The life
of the Illuminated is not an aimless, insipid, unattractive life.
Nothing that is truly good is denied him, whether it be for

enjoyment or for profit. All things are his if he will use them for a right and noble purpose in order that he may benefit himself and others.

In order that man may reach the highest, he must follow two lines of development. He must perfect both body and soul. Could he perfect body alone, free it from sickness and death, he would be no more than a perfect machine. In order to be more, than a perfect instrument, he must perfect the Inner Man, the Soul, and, through its perfection, come into direct personal touch and communion with the Father. He must follow a useful life, he must live according to the Divine Plan, according to the teachings that come through the instrumentality of those who have lived in harmony with both natural and divine law.

How is communion with the Godhead to be established?

This comes through fellowship with God, through daily communion with Him, through a companionship directly with the Father, a companionship not dreamed of by the multitudes. This fellowship is established more easily than man generally thinks. It results in a holy communion with God, the Father, which raises man gradually to the very highest. The best method for establishing such communion is through heart prayer in the Silence, by means of Sacred Mantrams. Sacred Mantrams, definitely formed with a definite purpose in view, and held in the heart to the exclusion of all else, will help man gradually to come into communion with the Father.

This is not accomplished at once. The child that is just beginning to talk is not understood by the parent, nor does the child understand the parent though the parent speaks plainly to the child. Nevertheless, our heart prayer, though imperfect, is understood by the Father; while we, not comprehending the divine language, do not understand the Father at first though He speaks plainly to us. But, if we are faithful to our prayer, gradually the heart comes into harmonious communion with the Father, and we will receive the heavenly music and will comprehend what the Father says to the Son. Thus is man and lids God brought into communion and fellowship.

Thus, in time, does man attain perfection of body and free himself from sin, sickness, and death. Thus, in time, does he attain perfection of soul and the Sublime Consciousness, consummation of the divine plan. It is these very things, the laws and the methods that underlie perfection of body and soul, which the Illuminati teach mankind through Soul Science, the Way to Immortality.

# THE WAY TO LIFE AND IMMORTALITY

## CHAPTER FIVE

## ONLY THE LIFE OF DEATH LEADS TO DEATH

The history of all inanimate things, as well as of the vegetable, animal, and human kingdoms, is the history of evolution.

In so far as the ordinary life of all things is concerned, the theory of evolution is correct. But evolutionists, as a rule, fail to take into consideration one important point, namely: the fact that man, having been given free-will (no matter by whom, whether by God or by himself), has the privilege of working in harmony with the laws of nature; and, when he awakens to this fact, he is no longer bound by the law of evolution, nor is he held back by it, but, by cooperating with it, he may outstrip it by far in the end. In order to work in harmony with the law of evolution, yet transcend its results, man must understand the greater law, that of Interior Development; and, by making use of this power, he is enabled to accomplish in one lifetime as much as the law of evolutionary progress could accomplish in thousands of years.

Thus, when man awakens from the deadening influences of the carnal self, and begins to recognize his great powers, he sets in motion new laws (or rather, laws that were heretofore unknown to him); and, instead of being a pawn in the grasp of the law of evolution, he becomes a master and works in harmony with, yet superior to, the law of evolution. By working thus, life becomes an unfoldment, a growth, in which he himself has conscious share. Whereas, without his voluntary cooperation, he is pushed forward merely because it must needs be so; for the law of progress forces him to advance, though slowly, whether he wills it so or not.

The Law of Interior Unfoldment is not new to man. It is not an invention or a discovery of modern times, nor is it the product of a fanatical imagination. It is a Law that has been known to the Masters of all ages. The Ancient Egyptians made use of it in the training of their priests. Every Neophyte in the Ancient Priesthood was developed and trained under this Law. By Egyptian Priests, who perfectly understood the Law of Development and Interior Unfoldment as well as the law of evolution, was Jesus trained unto Mastership; and for this reason he became the great Master and Teacher of mankind.

It is freely admitted that the law of evolution may accomplish what the Law of Conscious Development accomplishes. But the fact remains that, by following the Law of Conscious Development, man accomplishes in one short lifetime what nature and her laws working alone would require thousands of years, aye, possibly cycles.

This fact is illustrated in the animal kingdom, which, unless man takes a hand, is under the law of evolution. Any animal would serve as an illustration; but, to be specific, take the common hen. Allow her to run freely and to mate as she pleases, and there will be practically no improvement in her progeny within a period of thirty years. But let the man who understands the laws that concern the improvement of species take charge of the hen and mate her according to the laws of development, and in less than ten years he will produce the finest and most highly developed stock. This simply means that, in the improvement of species, man does not blindly depend on the laws of evolution, but that while working in harmony with them he makes use of a higher law, the Law of Development.

It is the same with man, If left to nature and her laws of progress, it is possible that he may, through the space of aeons and cycles, become a Soulified being. But, if he awakens to the possibilities of his destiny, and if, through working in harmony with the universal laws of progress, he makes voluntary use of the Law of Conscious Development or Interior Unfoldment, he may, in a comparatively short time, attain the Divine Consciousness.

The free choice belongs to man. This is the age of Illumination. It is an age in which the truth is being spread among mankind. The infinite possibilities of man's nature are being clearly pointed out to him. He is taught that instead of being a slave, "a worm of the dust," he has within himself the germ of Godhood, and that all he needs to do is to live in harmony with natural and divine laws. If he does this faithfully and conscientiously, he may be free from sickness and eventually be free from death.

Even those who consider Jesus merely as a great philosopher, and not as being in very truth the Son of God, can well afford to heed his instructions regarding the Law of Conscious Development and Interior Unfoldment. Even those who think slightingly of the Sacred Scriptures will do well to adopt for their own standard the doctrine that culminates in victory over death and the grave.

"O death, where is thy sting? O grave, where is thy victory?"

This expression is not a mere literary device, nor is it a fanciful theory. Rather, it expresses ultimate truth. After the flesh has been overcome, after the soul has arisen free and in glory from the experience men call death, then it is apprehended as indeed true that in death there is no sting, in the grave there is no victory.

This exclamation would have no value in itself to mankind had it not been demonstrated that death has no terror for those who have obeyed the Law of Unfoldment, that there is no death for the free, enlightened, illumined Soul. Even then, its value would have been negative but for the fact that the Master Jesus demonstrated the fruits of living in harmony with the Law of Unfoldment, and that he was able, through his own life, both to demonstrate to mankind the truth of the Law and to prove that obedience to the Law brings the legitimate fruits of obedience. Aye, even then, the teaching would be negative but for another fact- Jesus taught that, as he had done, so is it possible for all men to test the efficacy of living in obedience to the Law of Spiritual Unfoldment, and to prove the power of the Christ over sin, death, and the grave.

The true life of man is a life of interior Unfoldment- unfoldment from one degree, of being to another, a continuous unfoldment, which leads from carnality and selfishness upward to the plane of Godhood and Christship. Startling as this doctrine may seem, yet, nowhere in the Scriptures, nowhere in the philosophies, is there to be found a single statement contradictory to this principle; but everywhere, on every hand, is found evidence of the truth of these statements.

True, there is on record this saying: "Man that is born of woman is of few days and full of trouble." In its literalness, this statement contradicts the doctrine of life, joy, and immortality. Advocates of Soul Science and the Illuminati principles, however, claim that man when he has awakened from the carnal nature and has accepted the Divine Law as his standard and is following the Law of Unfoldment is no longer to be spoken of as "man that is born of woman," but is truly "man that is born of God." In the process of unfoldment, his carnal nature and even his body have been changed into the finer, the electric, being, and has therefore been born again, born of God, and is free from the laws that previously bound him. "Man that is born of woman" is full of trouble. But man that is born of God is no longer full of trouble, because conditions previously thought of as sorrows he has learned to consider as valuable experiences of life, stepping stones to a greater and a higher law. As man born of God, lie is heir to Life, Light, and Immortality.

Through such principles do Soul Science and the Illuminati lead their disciples away from the realm of death, away from the belief that God is a God of death, unto the realm of Life and Immortality, and to the truth that our God is a God of life.

The law of death, the carnal life, leads only to death; and, in this realm, is man truly born of woman, of few days, and full of sorrow. All this, however, the awakened man changes, he throws off the shackles of disease and of death, the shackles of ignorance and of fear; and he stands boldly before God, the Life Giver, and demands the heritage that is his, the heritage of Life, Light, and Immortality.

The life of death leads only to death; but there is a higher, a greater life- a life that is free from the passions that kill, a life that gradually frees itself from the destroyers, anger and jealousy, and puts in their place, love and forgiveness.

One of the most important things for man to do on entering the higher life is to free himself from that destructive power, that "Red Light of Death," anger. Significant indeed is the saying of the ancient philosophers, "Him whom the gods would destroy they first make mad." Nor is it far from being a literal statement of truth. Anger falls the entire system- body, mind, and soul- with poisons, and brings death in its path. He who becomes angry loses the sense of judgment; and, while in anger, he does things which he would not otherwise do. So great is the poison generated by this passion that it has been known to kill outright through the disease called apoplexy. Moreover, a fit of anger in the mother has been known to poison her milk so thoroughly that it has caused the death of the child suckling at her breast. The first step therefore in the overcoming of sickness and death is to free the self of anger and a hasty temper; for this is the most destructive of all the passions, and is the foundation upon which all other destructive passions rest.

If this passion is so destructive, it is but reasonable to teach that it must be overcome in order to insure health of body, mind, and soul. Left unrestrained, it tends toward disease, unhappiness, and, ultimately, death itself. Furthermore, if man overcomes this deadly passion, he will be able, through the power thus acquired, to gain victory over all other destructive passions. He will, as a result, receive health of body, mind, and soul, and eventually reach Illumination and overcome the last great enemy.

Remember that to live the life of death is to be overcome by death. No child of man ever plays with fire for any length of time without being burned. And no man can play with the weapons of death without being claimed by death.

Of the vices, or the passions, that lead to death, anger has been named as the most deadly. But there are other kindred instruments of death to which the carnal man is heir. Among these are jealousy, envy, faultfinding, and harsh criticisms of the failings, real or supposed, of our fellow beings. All these passions, destructive in the extreme, have been called "the green passions"; because they produce a poison that is green in color, they give the aura a green tinge, the color of destructiveness.

The tendency to anger and impatience is well-nigh universal. Almost all mankind is in its grip. Ofttimes it finds a home even in those who are nearing the goal of Illumination. One who is on the path to Life and Immortality, although he may have overcome the passion anger or an obstinate temper, may yet be in the grip of that other insidious destroyer, the sin of faultfinding. He who has not mastered this passion- the tendency to find fault with the habits and the ways of others- has still a deadly enemy lurking within.

This is not to say that the teacher, or the guide, of a Neophyte should not tell him of weaknesses, and point out to him the best method of overcoming them. To do this is his duty. But, if a person is not the teacher of others nor in authority over them, then he has no right to criticize their actions. He has a greater work right at home- the task of mastering the passions that cause discomfort, disease, and death to himself.

To give place to any of the destructive passions, means that we are, for the time being at least, living the life of death. While we may be earnestly groping for the light, we are, nevertheless, in the clutches of the grim reaper. And it is only the life of death, the life of destructive passions, that leads to death.

Jesus came as a teacher of the truth; but he went further than this. Others before him, other great philosophers, had taught the truth. But Jesus lived the truth, he demonstrated the fact that his teachings were the truth. Moreover, he explicitly emphasized that the life as he taught it can be lived by all who truly desire to live it. He also demonstrated the power of the Christ over sin, death, and the grave.

But, says the critic, if Jesus taught that the enemy death could be overcome, why did he allow death to come to his body? Why did he not demonstrate power over the grave by preventing death from coming to him?

It must be remembered that no man takes the third step on the ladder of advancement before he has taken the second. There are two ways by which man may prove the power of the Christ over death. One is to purify and refine the body to such a degree that the soul may lay it down in death, leave it temporarily, then return and take it up again. The other is to prevent death from coming to the body- that is, to prove that death is unnecessary. The body may be so refined and purified that its essences blend with, and become one with, the soul. Thus, body and soul ascend, or are translated, to the heavenly spheres without the necessity of the body's passing through the ordinary stages of disintegration.

Jesus could not demonstrate these two ways at the same time. He could demonstrate only the one or the other. And, as mankind was in ignorance concerning the practical features of immortality, he had to demonstrate the lesser first. Thus, he proved that the Soul lives even after the death of the body and that it may claim the body as an instrument of communication on the human plane even after the experience called death.

The seeker must bear in mind that it had long been prophesied that one was to come who would be able to give the life of the body, and, that, after a certain length of time, a time long enough to prove that the body was dead, he could take it up again. Jesus fulfilled this prophecy.

Again, the seeker must remember, Jesus prophesied that a time was to come in which man could do even greater things than he himself had done, a time in which man would demonstrate that death of body is unnecessary. Man may so live in harmony with natural and divine law that the body itself, together with the soul, may reach Immortality, and death will be unnecessary.

The Illuminati and Soul Science teach this truth and the way to its fulfillment. They boldly and clearly claim that, if the teachings are faithfully followed, the saying of Jesus will be fulfilled, and man will eventually overcome the last great enemy death. But let it be emphasized that such power as this is not developed in a short time or by any crude, haphazard methods. No claim is made that all mankind may attain unto this power during this one incarnation, or even during any one incarnation. The majestic oak is not grown in a day or a night, neither is an Illumined Soul developed in a single life period. The gate of death must be passed through many times before man can assume power over its keeper.

Let it be remembered that the carnal life, the life that indulges in deadly passions, alone leads to death. The life of virtue and constructive habits leads to Peace, Light, and Immortality.

## CHAPTER SIX

### TRUTH- AT FIRST, SEEMS HARD

The study of history reveals that every age has had its philosophers, Masters, Initiates, Saviors, who, having denied the self and followed the truth until they had reached Illumination of Soul, gave to the people the truths they had learned- truths gained not from books, but from experience and from actual living.

Move than this, history reveals the mistake of many men and women, who were attracted to these philosophers or teachers under the false impression that they might themselves attain Mastership without living the life that leads to Mastership. They desired to come into possession of such power and such knowledge as these philosophers and Masters possessed; but they were not willing to live the life that is required in order to gain possession of these powers. They had the mistaken notion that it is possible to obtain wisdom and power while still following a life of sin and death. In their foolish and carnal minds, they thought it possible to come into possession of truth, wisdom, understanding, power, and all other desirable things, by simply believing, or by a mere formal faith. They failed to recognize the fact that man cannot come into possession of anything legitimately, no matter what its nature, unless he is willing and ready either to work for it or to deny himself in some way or to do that which is required in order to receive.

Truth, in the beginning, seems hard. Truth says, Thus shalt thou do in order to receive. And, unless we are willing to accept the dictates of Truth and Wisdom, we shall not receive, rather, we cannot receive. For Truth and Wisdom and Power set their own price; and only he receives who pays the price in full in advance.

Indeed, it is possible to gain possession of some powers

through might, but they turn to bitter fruit in the end. No man can retain that which he did not receive legitimately. If he attempts to get and to hold in any illegitimate way, although he may enjoy possession for a time, the final results are always undesirable.

Thus, it has been the record of all times that there are those who think to gain possession of Truth, Wisdom, and Power, by some easy method, "by climbing up some other way." They go to a great Master and demand of him Truth, Wisdom, and Power. They listen attentively to his instructions, and then try to use the truth without living it. They gain a superficial comprehension of the Master's words, and undertake to apply it to life's needs, only to find that it evades their grasp, it is not theirs.

Truth belongs to him alone who earns it by the price of becoming. Truth is not an acquisition gained through mere intellectual effort. Knowledge of truth is the result of becoming, the result of being, the result of living in harmony with the laws of truth. Knowledge of truth is the result of Interior Unfoldment. It is the natural result of spiritual growth.

The true teacher or Master understands these things. He knows that truth cannot be obtained in any superficial way. And when he places before the people the choice of two things- either to live and to have or not to have- people turn away from him and seek elsewhere. They believe that there is some easy path to possession; but, alas, they find when life is spent that they were in quest of that which does not exist, and that the Law is absolute, which says, "Thus must thou do, if thou desirest to possess."

In the time of Jesus, it was not different from the previous centuries, centuries when Egypt was great, when its Priests ruled the world, and ruled it well, when men thought more of God and His blessings than they did even in the time of Jesus. And when the Master Jesus taught that physical death is unnecessary, the people would not believe it. Many of the disciples, those who had witnessed the wonderful works of the Master, turned and said, "This is a hard saying. Who can hear it?"

And why? Simply because they were not ready or willing to accept the great truth. The race belief could not even accept Immortality of Soul, or life after death of the body, how much less was it able to accept the doctrine that advocates immortality of body? Thus, the people turned away from Jesus and from his teachings. And, on account of this unbelief, this turning away, this refusal to accept the truth because it seemed hard and demanded something of them, they missed not only immortality of body but immortality of Soul as well.

Nor is it different in the present day. Many come to the Illuminati for instructions who already believe in the Immortality of the Soul; but they are unwilling to apply the teachings to their own needs. They are unwilling to live in obedience to the Law of Interior Illumination, and in their own experience to prove the Soul's reality. They demand some outward manifestation of power, aye, even demand a vision of the Heavenly Fire before they are willing to obey the heavenly vision.

In this, they forget the fact that the laborer is not paid before he has labored. They forget that God forces no man either to accept or to believe, that Lie forces no man to do, but that He gives all men free-will to do as they please, although He attaches the penalty of not doing, as well as the reward of doing. It is a fact that God forces no man to accept the Divine Truth, He forces no man to seek Immortality or freedom from disease. Yet it is equally a fact that He gives no man that which he has not earned. Neither does He show man signs and wonders in order to make him believe and live. On the contrary, He plainly teaches through the Masters and the Initiates that man should not seek for signs and wonders, but that he must *live* and *be*.

Again and again did Jesus try to teach the multitude that

physical death is unnecessary. But, in the end, he found that none would accept the hard saying. They simply left him and followed those who showed them an easier way of living. Even those who were continually with the Master found it difficult to accept the doctrine of immortality of the body. They found it impossible to comprehend the teaching that the Master was to lay down his body and take it up again, demonstrating without a doubt that there is no death to those that live the life.

At the end, when the multitudes had forsaken him, he attempted to teach the truth to his own disciples by saying, "Verily, verily, I say unto you, if a man keep my words, he shall not see death."

This is indeed a hard saying. This is the saying which the multitudes, aye, even the few, were not ready to accept in the time of Jesus. Nor will they accept it at the present time.

An easy saying indeed, that man may obtain and possess through mere belief even though continuing in a life of carnality and selfishness. No such saying did the Master Jesus ever utter. A belief that permits one to live the life of sin, ignorance, and error is not a true belief. That only deserves the name of faith which stimulates activity and endeavor to realize the fruits of faith. Faith is indeed necessary, but living according to the requirements of faith is also necessary. "Keeping the word" is necessary in order to obtain the results of the promise, which are, freedom from disease, ultimately freedom from death, an Immortality that includes both body and soul. Much, however, remains to be accomplished and realized in man's experience before immortality of body and soul can be attained. Even to overcome the race belief in the necessity of death is a wonderful achievement.

In its highest phase, life is an unfoldment. First of all, man is of the earth, earthy, and, from the earth, receives his strength. The rose, also, is of the earth, and from the earth receives its strength. But the rose has no power of choice, no power to resist the law that demands it to become something more than a bush of thorns. The rose is under natural law, which is under, and in obedience to Divine Law. And the rose must fulfill its destiny.

Though man is a prototype of the rose, he has free- will to accept the Law of Destiny or to reject it. For this reason, the vast multitudes go no further than the bush-of-thorn state. They are of the earth, earthly, and will not accept the truth. Nor will they live the life that enables them to pass through the stages that lead to a rose in full bloom. Gradually must they each one pass through the stages of growth that correspond to the parts of the rose bush. The stalk within must come forth. The bud must appear on the stalk. The bud must open into a full blown rose. In the case of man, the rose must remain open without the falling of petals and leaves. Man becomes an Illuminated, Immortal, God Conscious being.

This is the Law. It is a hard saying. Few are willing to accept it. It is a truth nevertheless, a truth that all may accept and reap the rewards of living in harmony with it. It will bind Immortality of Soul to those who accept it now; and, eventually, it will result in immortality of body and soul to those who overcome the race belief that death is a necessity, and who substitute in its place the conviction that our God is a God of life and the Giver of Life, Light, and Immortality.

What is the argument of the multitudes against the doctrine of immortality of the whole man?

The same today as in the time of Jesus, "Abraham is dead, and the prophets. Is man greater than these?"

Because man has died and continues to die, is no proof that it is necessary to die. Because, once upon a time, it was necessary to carry freight by means of horse and cart, is no reason that it cannot now be carried either by boat or by a system of rails.

# THE WAY TO LIFE AND IMMORTALITY

But, before freight was actually transported by modern methods, only the very few would accept the possibility of its being done in any other way than that to which they were accustomed. And, when the better way was finally proved and demonstrated, even then, by the many, it was regarded the work of the evil one. So hard is it for man to accept the new, though better way! No wonder it is hard for man to believe that anything but death is in store for him, so strong are the fetters of a long-standing race belief!

The multitudes demand signs and wonders. They will not accept the truth unless demonstrated in some miraculous manner. And, even then, when a man, freed from the race belief in death, begins to live according to the truth, the vast numbers will say, "Others have lived to good old age and then died, and so will he die." Thus, it will be centuries before the doctrine fully and freely taught by Jesus and the other philosophers will be accepted. In the meantime, the few will accept the life that leads to immortality of Soul. In time, they return to the earth to demonstrate the life that leads to immortality of body. Eventually, the final victory is won.

In the beginning, truth is hard to accept; and to follow the truth is also hard in the beginning. But, when man does accept the truth and begins to live it, and when the results of such living begin to show, then does he know that, although Truth is an exacting mistress, she is, nevertheless, one that gives ample returns for her exactitude.

"Keep my word, and ye shall never see death." This is not merely the teaching of Jesus but it is the divine command. Live the life. Live in harmony with the Divine Law, and then you will reap the benefits, the rewards, of such living.

But this we must understand and always bear in mind, that just as belief of itself is not sufficient, so is right living of itself insufficient. For, were living alone sufficient, then the animal of the field, living in harmony with nature, would have continuous life. But such is not the case. Faith and living are both necessary. Neither can be complete by itself. Living makes the possibility possible. Belief, or faith, so charges, magnetizes, or Aethizes, the Soul that it, having become God Conscious, raises the vibrations of the body, become pure through right living, to the Immortal plane.

For this reason, even many who have followed the path, and lived the life, though receiving Immortality of Soul, yet had to pass to the Beyond in order to realize immortality of the entire being, and this, simply because the mind and consequently the soul accepted the race belief that death is necessary in order to reach final immortality. And this belief, in spite of right living, made death of body necessary for them.

Thus, the Illuminati in their Soul Science, the Way to Immortality, teach that neither faith nor right living alone is sufficient in order to reach the highest goal of achievement, but that understanding of truth and faith. in the truth as well as living in harmony with the truth are necessary in order to know as the Gods knew and in order to reach final immortality.

Unlike other doctrines regarding immortality, the Illuminati do not teach that man, in attaining the final goal, loses his individuality and once again becomes part of the Godhead. They teach definitely and emphatically that man becomes an absolute, conscious individuality, free from all that is carnal and gross, like God, though not God.

Nor is this doctrine of the immortality of the whole man without examples. There have been those who walked with God- that is, had faith in God and in His promises and lived accordingly- who were taken body and soul, into the high heavens, and did not taste of death. Of these are Enoch, Elijah, and Moses, the great Law Giver. These believed as the ancient Priests taught. They believed in the word of God, in His promises. Through this belief and through the life they lived, they were able to fulfill the promises made by God.

So can all men do. But it is necessary for the hard truth to be believed, for the hard saying to be accepted. It is imperative that man shall not run after signs and wonders, after manifestations of others. It is imperative that he shall be the actor instead of being acted upon as a machine is acted upon by a master intellect, and that he shall become the Son of God through faith and through works, through belief and through living according to his belief.

God's Law is eternal. It is the Divine Law, absolute and never failing. Though we may think of this Law as a hard truth, nevertheless, when we become willing instruments, we find that it is not a hard life to live, that it is only seemingly so. It may be hard in the beginning, but we will soon learn that no good thing is forbidden to man.

To repeat: the perfect life is first of all faith accompanied by works. But we must be on our guard lest our faith becomes centered in personalities, which at best have weaknesses; and, if we are not ever watchful, we will judge them by their weaknesses and forget their strength. The perfect life is a life of service. It is not mere belief, a negative condition of existence, but, first and last, a courageous struggle to be. Finally, life is a growth, a be-coming, an unfoldment- a growth that begins on the material plane, gradually reaching the state of consciousness in which we realize that the carnal life is not the true life, finally leading to the state of consciousness in which the individuality merges into, and identifies itself with, the Divine yet retains its individual consciousness and identity. Thus, man becomes an immortal, deathless being, Son of the living God. Such is the destiny of man. Such a standard do the Illuminati teach. Soul Science points out the Way to Life, Light, and Immortality of the entire man.

## CHAPTER SEVEN

## MANS DUTY IS TO GLORY GOD

A question of importance is whether God, in creating man or anything else, did so with the intention of destroying the product of his creation. Or, put the question thus; do we, though at present but finite beings, create a thing with the intention of destroying it.

Search ourselves as we will, we come to the one conclusion that in making anything we do it because it seems good to do so, either for our own benefit or for the benefit of another. Moreover, having given it existence, we do not think of destroying it; though, at times, as our knowledge increases, we may desire to change or to improve our handiwork. If finite man in his efforts is prompted by altruistic motives, must it not be the more true that God, being infinite and having created all things perfect, does not desire to destroy his workmanship nor to make changes in it except such changes as come through normal, natural growth? This general statement being admitted as true, we must conclude that it is not the divine plan and purpose for either the soul or the body of man to be destroyed.

Why, then, is the body of man subject to death and decay?

To this there is but one rational answer. Because man, through disobedience to the divine command to become like God, makes it impossible for the body to continue existence; and, in this way, he himself and not his Creator is responsible for death of body or for mortality of soul. If this reasoning is correct (and who can question it?) we can come to but one conclusion- that is, the body of man was not created by God in order to be destroyed, nor was the soul destined by divine plan to eternal torment, neither did the divine purpose predetermine that either soul or body should be blotted out of existence.

To give a positive statement: man is created in the likeness of the Creator, endowed with the Creator's attributes and faculties. It is the divine purpose that he shall develop his inherent qualities in obedience to the Divine Law and that he shall so live as to become like God, his Creator, in every way. Furthermore, it is the divine purpose that he shall so live that the body may become pure and holy, truly a temple of the living God.

This it is to glorify God- so to live that the soul may reflect the Divine Image through a life of humble service, so to live that the body may become a temple wherein God may take up His permanent abode. This is the duty of man. This is the end and the aim of life. Further also, to glorify God results in happiness, peace, and contentment. When man comes to understand this principle and to live in harmony with the divine standard set for him, then will life here on earth become what it should be, what God intended it to be. This is the culmination, the ultimate goal, of glorifying God- to attain immortality of body and soul.

Nor is this doctrine contradictory in any way to Illuminati principles elsewhere advocated. It has long been taught that man may so live as to attain Illumination and Immortality of Soul, and Consciousness of God while in the flesh. This attainment is the result of a long-continued process that extends, it may be, through lives on earth oft- repeated. At the experience called death, the soul, having attained self-consciousness in partial degree, passes to the soul realm to remain for a time, with the privilege of returning to earth and completing the work that must be accomplished while in the flesh. This, the Law of Reincarnation, has been clearly explained as the method by which man advances on the Path to Christhood and Consciousness of Immortality. These principles are by no means contradictory to the doctrine of immortality of body and soul. They are, rather, stepping stones along the way, which lead to the higher, fuller doctrine of immortality of the whole man. They are subordinate to, yet in harmony with, the doctrine of complete immortality.

The doctrine of complete immortality advances the standard that the soul of man may find its heaven, its millennium, here on earth without going forth and without returning. The ideal of working for a far-off heaven, of hoping to attain peace and happiness in the far-off future is no longer attractive to mankind. To look forward to a state of being in the Beyond or in time to come, which the soul of man shall attain after death and there enjoy, ceases to satisfy. Men desire to attain the knowledge, the wisdom, and the power that shall enable them to overcome ignorance, sin, and disease here and now. They desire to become victors now and to realize that they are now on the Path to Mastership. Men need to realize that today is a part of the Hereafter, that today is a link in the chain of Eternity, that today determines the status of tomorrow.

Men are beginning to understand that disease is the result of ignorance, error, and sin, that illness is the result of disobeying, or of living contrary to, some law of health. It is becoming more and more a prevalent idea that life in the soul realm, life in the Beyond, is merely a continuation of the present life. As we are now, so shall we be then. The desires that hold the body now will hold the soul where there is no body. The habits that enchain and enslave on the earth plane will bind and hamper on the soul plane. Such ideas as these are becoming every day more deeply ingrained in the race consciousness That the present determines the future is even now a race conviction. That ignorance, error, sin, disease- aye, even death- are conditions to be overcome, not conditions which demand passive resignation, is fast becoming a race belief.

The race consciousness has too long been content with a religion that has unduly emphasized helpless submission to a divine providence, passive resignation to a Higher Will, blind surrender to an unseen ruling power. But the tide has turned. Such teaching ceases to give comfort. The tendrils and the "feelers" of the race consciousness are turning toward the light and are reaching out for a positive, active, virile religion. The multitudes are seeking light and true understanding. They are seeking the truth that will guide them aright. They are tired of being admonished to be submissive and resigned. They are tired of being the plaything of unseen forces. They hunger to become creators and actors and directors. They hunger for the truth and the wisdom and the power that will enable them to become creative agents and active forces.

On all sides are evidences of ignorance, error, sin, disease, suffering, sorrow, and death. Under mysterious and unaccountable "ministrations of providence," man has known no better philosophy than to bow in submission, and to "bide a wee, and dinna fret." But this ceases to satisfy. Now he asks. Why. Now he seeks the cause of "painful ministrations of providence"; and, having discovered the cause, he seeks to put forth active measures to prevent, and to remove causes. Hitherto, he has glorified God by a negative, blind, inert submission. Now he seeks to glorify God by the use of conscious, deliberate, definite, painstaking effort to fulfill the Divine Purpose and to realize the Divine Plan. Hitherto, he has glorified God by saying, "Nevertheless, not my will, but thine be done." Now he seeks to glorify God by saying: "I will that thy Will be done through me. I will to become an active instrument in thy hands. I put forth conscious, deliberate effort to direct the Christ Potencies into channels of useful service."

The many have been saying, "We want to believe; but you must first show us some manifestation which will enable us to believe." The day is well-nigh at hand, however, when the demand for outer demonstration of truth will be changed into the determination, "I will live the life that leads to inner realization of truth." It is not reasonable to expect the doctrine of full and complete immortality to be accepted immediately and in a short time and by great numbers. The blotting out of the old belief and the establishment of a new in the race consciousness is at best a slow, gradual process. Nor is it necessary to look at the ultimate in order to accept the higher truths. One may accept truth that tends eventually toward the ultimate without striving after or even desiring the ultimate. One may not desire bodily immortality, one may not be attracted by the thought of heaven on earth. But who is there in the vast multitudes that does not desire freedom from disease and suffering? Who is there that does not desire an understanding of causes? Who does not desire freedom from ignorance, error, sin, and suffering? To desire even this, and to accept the truth that leads to this freedom, is an important step toward breaking down long-standing race beliefs and establishing in the race consciousness higher and purer motives.

True sincere desire for freedom from ignorance, error, sin, disease, and suffering causes one to accept the truth, and to live the life, that lead to freedom from ignorance, error, sin, disease, and suffering. Living in harmony with the truth that sets free necessitates obeying the Divine Law, the Law that leads ultimately to full immortality, to believe the truth in regard to the cause of undesirable conditions in life, and to live in such wise that desirable conditions shall become ours, puts one in harmony with, and enables one to cooperate with, the Law that leads to the highest goal, even though one may not be striving to reach the highest goal, aye, even though one may not consider the ultimate as at all desirable.

We must remember that the Law is, that the Law includes and covers all that is, that the lesser is no less and no more than the beginning of the greater. For as above, so below; as below, so above; as the lesser, so is the greater. To accept the lesser and to strive after it, clears the way for the greater. Thus, step by step, degree by degree, the race belief advances, and the race consciousness seeks higher planes, and the race conscience takes on purer motives and loftier ideals, until, eventually, belief in full immortality is accepted by mankind as the highest, and, withal, the most desirable, goal.

And what means obedience to the Law, both natural and divine:

It means ultimately a perfect body. It means a perfect, creative, virile mind. And the two working in harmony produce the perfect Soul, the Christos, the Soul that is conscious of Christhood and Mastership.

Some object to the word Christ, saying that the world has had enough of the Christ teachings, and that there is a demand for something more advanced. Such must understand that there is nothing greater than the Christ Principle. Though another name may be used by which to designate it, yet the power that the Christ Principle represents, ever remains a mighty reality, the most powerful factor known to man. Man may call himself the reincarnation of an ancient god or even a new incarnation direct from the Godhead, yet the eternal element in his being is ever the same, no matter what name may be applied to it. No man has yet lived to the full the teachings of Jesus, the Christ. Therefore, the world can cite no perfect example to represent the teachings. Consequently, the claim that they have lost their power is to manifest gross ignorance in respect to the truth contained in them, and simply indicates superficial knowledge. The Christ teachings, in their mystical sense, have never been really understood and believed, much less have they ever been lived and demonstrated.

What then is it to become a Christ Soul? What is it to know the Christ, not as a personality, but as the life of man?

To know the Christ is to have attained Illumination of Soul. To become the Christ Soul means that, through a system of living in obedience to natural and divine law, man attains consciousness of the Christ, and of God, the Father. To have reached this state of being is to have freed the self of grosser passions, is to have made the body whole. Moreover, it is the state of consciousness in which the soul says with Jesus, "I am the resurrection and the life." In this state of being not only does man live, but he lives on a higher plane than heretofore. Born not only of his mother, in pain and in sorrow of the flesh, but born of God into a, higher state of being, he can truly say, "I am the resurrection and the life." The divine spark of a soul within him has been nurtured and fed until it has become a brilliant Flame of Love, Understanding, and Power. He has seen the Fire, he has beheld the heavenly vision. Does he not know that he shall surely live and not die?

All this belongs to him who has believed the truth and has lived in harmony with the truth and has obeyed the Law of truth. Even though man may still cling to the race belief in the necessity of death, yet Illumination of Soul and Consciousness of Immortality of Soul, together with the fruits of such consciousness, are indeed desirable. Whatever may be one's thought in regard to bodily immortality, Consciousness of Immortality of Soul is a most desirable attainment. It allies one to God, the Father, Creator of all- "Him in whom we live and move and have our being."

It was the Christ Principle in Jesus that gave utterance to the words, "He that liveth and believeth in me shall never die." This saying gives no ground for centering our faith in a personality. It gives no basis for the doctrine that belief in the historic character of Jesus or even belief that he was the Son of God in itself insures salvation of soul. He that liveth and believeth as Jesus lived and believed, he that liveth and believeth in the Christ- he shall never die. Such is the promise. If we live and serve humanity as Jesus did, not merely in slavish imitation of him, but in obedience to the Divine Law which ruled his life and which also centers in our own consciousness, then we shall find life eternal; and, freed from erroneous race beliefs, we shall not know death.

# THE WAY TO LIFE AND IMMORTALITY

Man has been following the letter and not the spirit of the Law. Man has been believing in the personality of Jesus. Some indeed have believed in the existence of the Soul, and in the Christ; but this belief, though good, has availed nothing. Even this, though a correct belief so far as it goes, can bring no satisfactory results. To believe in the personality of some historic character, no matter how divine the character may be, is not sufficient. The belief that brings results in one's life is belief in the Law demonstrated by the personality of some ideal historic character. Have faith in the Law by which and through which that particular personality was enabled to reach Divinity and Immortality of Soul, and to become conscious of God, the Father- this is the Divine command.

This is to glorify God- to establish faith in a Divine Principle, a Divine Promise, a Divine Command, a Divine Law. This is the significance of the mission of the Master Jesus. In his personality and in his individuality was exemplified and manifested the Divine Law, in order that, through this exemplification, the Law might be accepted by others as a guide. It is for others to obey the Law as he obeyed it. It is for others to believe the truth and to live the truth as he believed and lived, and, through such obedience and through such a life, to reap the rewards and the fruits.

The soul is deathless as is He deathless who created the soul. God cannot manifest without a medium through which to manifest. Man is the medium through which God manifests Himself. Likewise, the soul cannot manifest without a medium through which to manifest. The body of man is the medium through which the soul manifests. It is just as reasonable to claim that God, in order to save Himself, must destroy man through which He manifests as to claim that man must, in order to save the soul, destroy the body through which the soul manifests. God destroys no man. Man, through disobedience to the Divine Law, may destroy himself. In like manner, death of the body is not a necessity; but man may, through disobedience, cause its death. Not that anything is gained through its death, not that the soul will be more sublime or more advanced. Nevertheless, because of the race belief in the necessity of death, he takes it for granted that the body must die. Consequently, it does die. In time to come, however, belief in the possibility of Life Eternal will become so established in the race consciousness that man will take it for granted that death of the body will not be his. Consequently he need not know death of body.

Death of body does not add to exaltation of soul. On the contrary, the more man purifies the body, the more perfect the body becomes through obedience, the more does he glorify God in the Highest. And, in like manner, in proportion as he purifies the body and perfects it, in that degree is the soul exalted and made purer and cleaner until, after Baptism with Fire, it reaches to heaven and comes into conscious relationship with the Creator.

Thus, it stands that, whether physical immortality is desired or not, it is the duty of man so to live as to glorify God and to bring the Soul to Illumination. In so doing, he is actually living the life that, if continued, ultimately results in complete and full immortality and places him on the plane of consciousness that says, "I am the resurrection and the life." The consciousness of Life Eternal he guards as a sacred trust and confesses to no man. But his life, in its fruits of service and good deeds, daily testifies to others of the power of the Christ Consciousness. This tends toward the perfection of the human race.

This is life, life in its higher and most holy manifestation. This is science. In every case in which the Law is faithfully obeyed, results are the same. This is philosophy. This is religion. It concerns not only the soul but the body as well. It is that which God has tried to teach His children, lo, these many ages.

Jesus, having become the Christ, demonstrated that life

remains even after death of body. He demonstrated to those who believed that man may so live as to retain consciousness, so live as to have more power, after the change called death. To demonstrate this fact was the culmination of his mission. But he taught that which is even greater, that which he could not himself demonstrate. He could demonstrate only the one truth, that life and consciousness of soul continue after death and that man may, through the Christ Power, take up the body after it had passed through the change called death. But he taught the greater truth, namely, that man may so live as to prevent death to the body, that man may find life eternal, life without change, life as God intended it to be. To demonstrate this possibility is to be classed among "the greater things" which Jesus said his followers should do.

"He that believeth and liveth in me"- that is, he who has faith in the God-given Law and who lives according to the Divine Law- shall be free from sin, disease, and ultimately, shall demonstrate power over the last great enemy death. Thus shall man glorify God by living the life God intended him to live, the end of which is happiness, peace, and contentment. This is the teaching of Soul Science, the Way to Life, Light, and Immortality.

## CHAPTER EIGHT

## GOD IS EVER WITH THOSE WHO ARE WITH HIM

If man rightly appreciated the saying, "God helps those who help themselves," he would make greater effort toward the accomplishment of the things he desires to accomplish. This saying means that God is with those who are with Him. Although He is not against those who are not with Him in thought and in deed, yet He is not able to help them.

In its literalness, this interpretation may seem to portray God as a personal being who arbitrarily refuses to help those who do not help themselves. The expression, however, is to be thought of, rather, as a literary cloak which covers a general, universal truth. Those who help themselves, by that very act, open their natures to receive the forces and the potencies of the Infinite. By that very attitude of mind, they admit into their being the qualities that make for success in the channels of their endeavor. By that attitude of mind, they come into harmony with the Divine Law of their own Being; and, in so far as they do truly help themselves, to that extent do they obey the law of their own Being.

It follows that the best way to help ourselves is to seek the Kingdom of God within our own Being and to cooperate with the Law of Divinity within ourselves. In the accomplishment of any worthy purpose, the first step of importance is to seek the Kingdom within, and there to receive instructions which will enable us to work in harmony with the Divine Law. Having received knowledge of truth and having faith in the promise that God helps those who help themselves, it remains to put forth effort in harmony with the knowledge received, and to work according to one's faith. This is to work in harmony with the Will of God. To work in accordance with the Divine Will is to be with God. And God, being just and absolute, can not do otherwise than be with us.

# THE WAY TO LIFE AND IMMORTALITY

The result will be that we shall, in the end, obtain those things which we desire, those things which we are putting forth effort to obtain. This is true, no matter what our desire may be, whether for health of body, mind, and soul, or for freedom from sorrow and suffering, or for Immortality of Soul, or for Immortality of Soul and body. To be sure, freedom from sorrow and suffering must come through the knowledge that things which ordinarily cause sorrow and suffering are experiences necessary to make us more nearly perfect. This knowledge of itself alleviates suffering and enables us to accept it with fortitude and to turn all experiences in life to good account.

In the effort to attain perfection we are not alone. For, on every side, there are those who are on the way to perfection, very many of whom have advanced to an appreciable degree of perfection in body, mind, and soul. Seldom, however, do we find one who is perfect in all three. But those who have partially attained perfection in any one department of life serve as examples and as inspiration to others. The perfect in body proves to us that perfection of body is a possibility in which all men may share. Perfection of mind or intellectual achievement proves that it is possible for others to be mentally perfect. Perfection of Soul, or Illumination of Soul, or Sonship with God, proves to us that all things are possible to him who honors the Christ in his own life and character.

One should, however, go a step beyond this, and aim at threefold perfection- perfection of mind, soul, and body. The Illuminati hold the standard of perfection in the three departments of man's nature, and the harmonious cooperation of each with the other. The ideal is unity out of the trinity, one through the three.

Through knowledge of the Divine Law and through obedience to it, we free the mind from those thoughts and those teachings which hamper, and which prevent it from greater achievement. In the place of undesirable thoughts and erroneous teachings, we feed the mind constructive, wholesome thoughts and ideals, which develop all three departments of man's nature. Through freeing the mind of conditions which hamper and bind it to earth, through the establishment of powerful, constructive thoughts, we build the healthy body, the enlightened mind, and the illumined soul.

God helps those who, seeing that His work is perfect in certain departments, follow the example of those who have attained. God helps those who apply to their own personality the principles and the laws demonstrated by those who have attained. Gradually and in natural order, the personality becomes the individuality, which, in turn, gives way to Sonship- Sonship with the Father. The fact that some have attained perfection is proof that others may attain. In the beginning, all things, including man, were perfect; but man, having free-will, has brought imperfection into the universe. But now again men are awakening to the truth; and, understanding the Divine Law, and seeing perfect works, they are beginning to pattern after them.

True, accomplishment is not in a moment. It will require time to bring about satisfactory results. But, unlike all else in nature, man can exchange the carnal self for the spiritual self within a comparatively short time. Even his body can be reconstructed, and every cell thereof replaced with a new one, within a period of less than one year. In animal life, to be sure, there is a constant replacement of old cells by new; but, in human life, there is the added responsibility of charging the new cells with thoughts of regeneration, perfection, and deathlessness. Nothing else in nature has such possibilities as has man. This in itself is indication of the mighty responsibility that falls upon him, a responsibility proportionate to the possibilities God has given him.

The main thing, at the present time, is to awaken man to his great possibilities, and to arouse in him an earnest desire to attain the highest of which he is capable. He must realize the fact that the life he is now living is not the true life. Nor is it the life that brings the greatest power and the greatest freedom from suffering and other undesirable conditions. The life of ease and sin and pleasure may, indeed, seem to be the easiest life. In reality, however, it is not the easiest. Man has been deluded by the thought that the downward road is easier to travel, that things which are evil are easier to do, that destructive habits are more pleasurable than constructive and power-producing habits. This, however, is far from true. This, like belief in the necessity of death, is a race delusion which has in fact no foundation.

There is another race error kindred to this which must be uprooted from man's nature, the error of thinking that all things which give pleasure and joy are of the evil one and must not be indulged in. Since man in normal condition is a pleasure-loving, joy-seeking being, he naturally and instinctively craves conditions which produce the sensation of joy and pleasure. Going to extreme in gratifying his fondness for pleasure, or indulging in sense-delights contrary to nature's laws, he has reaped the reaction, or the after-effects, of sorrow and suffering. Consequently, he concludes that those things which give pleasure and joy are in themselves wrong. This, too, is an erroneous conclusion. Sorrow and suffering are due, not to the gratification of sense-pleasure, but to excess or to abuse or to abnormal conditions. The falsity of thinking that joy-producing conditions are of the evil one must be eliminated from man's thought.

God helps those who help themselves. God helps those who try to eliminate from their minds false conceptions and erroneous standards. God is with those who try to free themselves from bondage to race errors.

The Illuminati teach that God looks upon results and ultimate effects, and that He judges from the outcome and from the final tendency. He has not endowed man with pleasure-loving inclinations for the sake of taunting him through non-gratification or for the sake of putting temptation in his way as a means of testing his strength. Things which give pleasure, joy, and happiness are not in themselves evil. The gratification of sense delights is not necessarily productive of pain and sorrow, nor is it necessarily an evil. The demands of the physical nature are in themselves legitimate. Aye, more than this, they are requisites of spiritual growth. They are agents of regeneration. They are necessary factors in refining and in purifying the physical organism, which in turn acts as a refining and purifying agency in development of soul.

Man must learn to help himself by seeking to root out of his nature the false impression that gratification of the senses is in itself sinful. God looks to see whether results are constructive or destructive, whether the end is sorrow, pain, or loss to the self or to any other creature. When results are good, constructive, and uplifting, there is no pleasure, no happiness, no enjoyment, which is prohibited, nor does it in any wise meet with the disapproval of the Creator. The understanding of this law, and a recognition of the fact that physical welfare and normal physical satisfaction are necessary to mental and spiritual welfare, gives to life a brighter hue and relieves the somber effects of a perverted religious standard. Life would look far different to the vast multitudes if they could comprehend the distinction between normal use of functions, which gives happiness, and abnormal or perverted use, which results in pain and regret. It is only man and his acts, his ignorance, and his foolish conception of life that bring pain, sorrow, and misery into the world. Life will seem worth the living when God helps man because he helps himself by eliminating from his thought false impressions and false standards.

God is not a Being that is trying to shoulder all the pain, sorrow, and suffering upon humankind. On the contrary, He is a Being who is trying to help man to perfection, to help him become truly man in order that he may become truly a god. It is the divine purpose that man, through evolving his own inherent possibilities, shall attain unto Godhood and Christship. The pain, sorrow, and suffering which man experiences in life are not to be traced to God in any other sense than that' He has given him free-will; and, through perversion and misuse of his faculties, man has brought sorrow and suffering upon himself and upon others. He who seeks wisdom that he may make intelligent use of his free-will is helping himself in such a way that he can truly receive the help of God. God is with him who seeks wisdom and guidance. God is with him who opens the channels of his being to the Divine Presence.

Through the past centuries, God has permitted, aye, even ordered, perfect beings, men become perfect, to pass through the world in order to teach men the perfect way. But mankind has refused to listen to the voice of these great teachers. The last of the great Initiates who came to the earth not only taught Immortality of Soul but even demonstrated the possibility of laying down the mortal physical body in death and of taking it up again at will. But it has required well-nigh two thousand years for man actually to comprehend this possibility. It has required these centuries to enable man to understand this mystery. Now he is beginning to comprehend that not mere faith in a great Master will bring results, but that it is necessary to have faith in the Law which the Master obeyed in order to attain Mastership, and that it is necessary to obey the Law even as he obeyed it. Man may have a faith that precludes the shadow of a doubt in a great Master. He may believe without wavering that another has attained Mastership, Godhood, and Christship. But what does this avail of practical value to man unless he realizes that it is according to the Divine purpose for himself and all men to attain the same state of Divinity?

This is a race error that must be overcome- the belief that the Master Jesus was a miraculous exception to the possibilities of human life, that he was God come to the earth in a manner that transcends human endeavor. This error must be supplanted by the conviction that the Master Jesus was a perfect illustration of what all men may attain by obeying the Law of Immortality as he obeyed it. He stands as a perfect example, saying clearly to all. What I have done ye may do. It is the divine will and purpose for all men to strive to attain such Mastership as Jesus demonstrated. Striving to attain Christship is to insure the Presence of God. The Divine Presence overshadows and helps those who cherish for themselves the ideal of Christship and Supreme Mastery. Man works with God and is with God and reaps actual results when. he strives to live a life of service to others in harmony with the Christ Ideal. Aye, even he is working with God and is with God and reaps actual results, who strives to free himself from bondage to erroneous race beliefs.

The Master Jesus did more than teach Immortality of Soul. He taught Immortality of body as well. But many centuries have been required to establish the plausibility of the doctrine of Immortality of Soul. So, also, many other centuries will be required to establish in the race consciousness the possibility of physical immortality. The race thought is thoroughly saturated with the belief that sin, suffering, sickness, sorrow, misery, and finally death are necessary. This belief is in every cell of the entire body. New cells in the process of rebuilding are charged with this same thought. Thus, body, mind, and soul are magnetized with thoughts of disease, suffering, fear, sorrow, and death. "As a man thinketh in his heart, so is he." Is it any wonder that years and even centuries are required to transmute race errors into race truths?

But the new age is at hand, the beginning is made. Belief in Immortality of Soul, in the Fatherhood of God, and in Conscious Sonship with the Father is thoroughly established in the minds of many. Many are beginning to think and to live in harmony with this conviction. The fact that physical refinement and purification are necessary to the spiritual growth that leads to Conscious Sonship with God is fully understood and accepted by many. Thus, through the advanced thought and the higher understanding of the many, the race consciousness is being rapidly tinged and colored with the bright hues of belief in Immortality of Soul. This proves that the time is ripe for spreading the doctrine of immortality of body. Only the few may be ready to comprehend and to accept it, but there must be a beginning sometime, somewhere, in the promulgation of every new aspect of truth. Those who are settled in their acceptance of Immortality of Soul are ready for the next step. Many are definitely meeting the requirements of a life that leads to Conscious Sonship with God. They are seeking manifestation of their own Sonship with the Father. They are practicing religion and philosophy in order to manifest to their own consciousness the Immortality of their own souls. Many have faced the Altar Fire and have gazed into the brilliant depths of their own Being, and, awe-inspired by the Divine Presence, have breathed upon their own consciousness the truth, "I am the Resurrection and the Life." Upon many the Dove of Peace has alighted. To many the Invisible Voice has uttered the words: "Thou art my beloved son in whom I am well pleased."

Such consciousness of the Divine Presence, such Realization of the Ineffable Light of Immortality, such manifestation of Life Eternal, belongs to themselves alone- a sacred trust, which can not be communicated to others, a sacred reality, which can not be imparted to the vast multitudes who cry out for signs and wonders. It is a truth of paramount importance that manifestation of the Immortality of the Soul can not be given to others, for the reason that man can not understand or see in others that which is not yet in himself. Though a man might have reached Illumination, though he might have brought forth his soul as a self-conscious entity, aye, even though the Holy Fire might become visible to those who have not yet reached Illumination, others would not believe it nor credit his personal testimony. They would consider it a delusion of the senses and not an actual fact. For this reason it is an absolute truth that those who demand of others a manifestation of the Soul, the Sacred fire, the Almighty God, are themselves yet in darkness and know neither the Soul nor God. For this reason- because of their own blindness and misapprehension of the truth- they demand signs and wonders, manifestations and proofs. Their own unbelief and their own unworthiness have prevented them from bringing into manifestation the Divine fire within themselves.

Unless we seek and find within ourselves, we are unable to understand, to see, and to comprehend that which is within others. Be it understood that men judge others not by what others are, but by what they themselves feel, and by what they themselves are within their own consciousness. It is a Divine Law that man can not understand that which he is not himself. He can not comprehend the forgiveness of the Infinite until he realizes forgiveness of others in his own heart. He can not comprehend that impartial love and good-will toward all creatures is a possibility until he realizes it in his own experience. In recognition of this Law, the Master Jesus taught: "Seek ye first the Kingdom of Heaven and all these things will be added unto you."

Thus, in proportion as God is with us, in proportion as we know Him and realize His presence, do we look for Him in others. Again, as we are of the world, carnal, and selfish, do we seek to find the same condition in others; and we can not understand how they can be better than we or comprehend more than we. Bear in mind that God is ever with those who are with Him. There is no restriction placed on this statement. Nor is there a limitation to the degree of "God with us." He who is beginning to awaken to the truth, he who is beginning to overcome the thralldom of race errors, he who is beginning to work in harmony with the Creator and His Laws, is just as great as he who has reached final redemption, final unfoldment. For, as is the beginning, so must the end be if the beginner persists faithfully in obedience to the Divine Law. The beginning leads to Sonship and Godhood.

It is such truths as these that Jesus came to shadow forth and to demonstrate to mankind. He stated clearly that the least of these is greater than John the Baptist. For those who are least have already made a start on the right way, the way that leads to Godhood; and, thus, they may in time surpass John the Baptist in a true spiritual sense.

Through the life of the Master Jesus, God proved that He is with man. Through the obedience of Jesus to the Divine Law, God proved to mankind that it is possible to demonstrate the fruits of faith and obedience. Through the power of the Christ in Jesus, God taught mankind. He expects man not only to do what Jesus did but even to do greater things. It must be remembered that Jesus was subject to race environment as are we. He was born in the race belief in the necessity of death. He was born even in the belief that there is no Immortality. But, through faith and through works, he was able to overcome the race belief in the necessity of death. He was able to demonstrate Immortality of Soul, and to instruct mankind in the Law that will enable him to demonstrate immortality of body as well as Immortality of Soul.

The Master Jesus illustrated by his life what it is to work with God and to be with God, what it is to have God as guide and helper. God can not be with those who are not with Him any more than Lazarus could go to the rich man, for there is a mighty, impassable gulf between. God can not manifest His Infinite Presence to those who claim to believe, but who in reality have no faith. There is a vast difference between profession and actual possession. God is with those who, in all humility, come to Him, asking for help, aye, even asking for faith- more faith and a purer faith. When the heart is sincere and earnest, even though it has but little faith, a true desire for necessary faith draws God to it, and opens the channels of the heart to receive an influx of faith from the Infinite Storehouse. God is with those who earnestly desire to be with Him and to work with Him in harmony with His Laws, even though their faith is weak and wavering. Let every hungry, tempest-tossed, wavering soul remember that God is with those who are with Him.

## CHAPTER NINE

## WHAT OF THE CRUCIFIXION OF THE FLESH?

A grievous race error is found in the doctrine that, in order to attain eternal life, it is necessary to crucify the flesh, and that salvation is impossible without crucifixion and denial of the flesh. This doctrine has been the means of holding back vast multitudes from accepting the teachings of. Masters and Philosophers.

In fundamental aspects, this doctrine contains much truth. But it has been grievously misunderstood and misrepresented until the misrepresentations and the errors growing out of it have, in the minds of the general public, supplanted the true doctrine.

From time untold, it has been thought that crucifixion of the flesh makes necessary the denial of all those pleasures which belong to the flesh. It tends toward strict, severe, unreasonable self-discipline. Only a few centuries ago, our puritan fathers denied their children the right to play, even the right to smile, on the sabbath day. Unreasonable though this may seem to us, to them it seemed right; and to play or to laugh on the sabbath day brought punishment to the child. In this, however, the parents were consistent; for what they denied their children they would not do themselves. There was no legitimate reason for such self-denial. It is a question whether our ancestors who were so strenuously careful of details in regard to sabbath observance gave the matter serious thought. They believed in strict observance of the sabbath because they had been taught to believe in it, and that was enough.

But we, of the new age, must reason and analyze, and know why an act is right or wrong. In the present day, it is not generally considered wrong to indulge in merriment and activity on the sabbath day. But are we supplied with a reason for so thinking, or are we taking our view for granted match as our ancestors did theirs?

Determining the right or the Wrong of an act in question is comparatively a simple matter. Let the first question be, Will the act hurt anyone, either the self or another? Let the second question be, Will the act benefit anyone, either the self or another? Reasoning along these two lines will readily satisfy the most sensitive conscience in regard to the right or the wrong of a doubtful proposition.

Another point, important because it enters into the consideration of many acts, is concerning whether the day on which an act is committed affects the act in regard to right or wrong. Is it right to do' a certain thing on one day or on six days, and wrong to do it on the seventh day?

In general, it may be said that what is actually wrong on the seventh day is likewise wrong on any other day. The Law of God is absolute in that it classifies wrong as wrong, and right as right. The Divine Law recognizes only two criteria for determining wrong and right. If an act, a thought, or a desire in any way results in injury to oneself or to another it is to be regarded as wrong. If it is free from injury, and results in benefit to the self and others, it is to be regarded as right. These two criteria are independent of days and seasons, time and place. That which is right to do on the sabbath is right for other days. That which is wrong to do on the sabbath is wrong for another day.

Just as our puritan fathers had conceptions of right and wrong, just as they recognized certain forms of crucifixion of the flesh, so, throughout the centuries, the multitudes have held to beliefs of many kinds- some of which are rational and praiseworthy, others of which are unreasonable and even detrimental to human welfare. The unreasonable and the erroneous have been associated with the reasonable and the true so intimately as to be regarded equally important with them. Consequently, in the minds of the multitudes, the errors and the falsities of the race belief in crucifixion of the flesh give the most prominent coloring to the doctrine, and make it unattractive or even obnoxious to them. It is not surprising, then, that the doctrine of the crucifixion of the flesh should, in the minds of the many, identify itself with an irksome self-denial which interferes with happiness and enjoyment of every description. No wonder the teachings of Masters and Initiates on this subject are rejected. At the very mention of the word, without investigation, it is taken for granted that crucifixion means painful repression, and merciless rigidity of discipline, and sanctimonious effacement of joy and naturalness.

That this is not a correct interpretation of crucifixion of the flesh is a fundamental principle of the Illuminati. That the doctrine, truly understood, admits of bright colors and pleasing outlines is a truth that receives emphasis among them. To reestablish the Christie significance of crucifixion in its simplicity and in its beauty is distinctly marked as one aim of the Church of Illumination. They would emphasize the bright side of the doctrine and crucifixion. They would disentangle the erroneous from the true, the irrational from the rational. This they would do, not by exercising priestly authority in laying down definite rules of right and wrong, not by specifying details for everyday use of all men alike, not by sitting in judgment over others- nay, far from it- but by defining general principles through which each one may determine for himself the correct or the incorrect disposal of matters which concern his own personal life.

Crucifixion is not to be identified with repression of naturalness and ease, nor with suppression of joy and merriment. Nor is it in any way inconsistent with pleasure and happiness, whether in the form of social functions, games, sport, and other kinds of wholesome recreation and diversion. Normal gratification of one's social nature, normal satisfaction of the demand for physical activity apart from labor and toil, reasonable indulgence in festivities and merry-making, stimulating interests which admit of variety along lines of art, nature, and music- all these are not only permissible but even advantageous to man's spiritual growth.

This postulate the Illuminati lay down with positive emphasis, that the rightness or the wrongness of a thought, desires or an act, is to be determined by its effects or its tendencies, whether it results in harm and injury to the self or to others or whether it results in benefit and profit to the self and to others. Any merriment or pleasure- aye, even any thought or desire- that brings pain, sorrow, suffering, harm, or injury to another human creature or to the participant is to be classed among "Things forbidden." Nor is there any other law under the sun that classes thought, desire, or act among "things forbidden." The reason for its being so classified is not that it falls in any particular category of things labeled "thus shalt thou not." It is so classified for the one simple, yet fundamental reason that it is productive of harm.

The Law that classifies as right those things which are productive of good and beneficence, and as wrong those things which are productive of harm and injury- this law concerns the body and conditions which affect the formation of the body. It concerns that which man partakes of as food and drink. It includes hygienic laws in every department of life. Many people who are devoutly conscientious in regard to the outer forms of worship and in regard to visible signs of correct conduct, are, nevertheless, woefully indifferent to hygienic conditions which vitally affect the welfare of body, mind, and soul. What natural laws, or the laws of health and efficiency, come under the category of "right and wrong" is a fact that fails to prick the conscience of many who are in other respects of irreproachable character. Yet these are the very points that the Illuminati would emphasize.

This is the foundation on which the Temple of Illuminati rears its structure. It builds around the corner stone of general principles and fundamental laws, which each devotee must learn to apply to his own needs as the mathematician handles his own instruments. Beauty and perfection in the mathematician's work are due to an exact comprehension of mathematical laws as well as to accuracy, precision, and delicacy in the guiding of instruments. Likewise, beauty and perfection of character result from correct knowledge of natural and divine law, by which one is enabled to exercise judgment and decision, delicate and precise and accurate.

In these points, the Illuminati depart from the well-trodden path of tradition and ancestral training. They regard natural law, or the laws of physical health and mental efficiency, as being co-equal with ethical and moral law. They place hygienic and dietary discretion on a par with social and moral uprightness. They extend the boundary lines of righteousness to include the practical aspects of dietetics, sleep, work, exercise, and other hygienic laws, as well as the principles of eugenics and sexual science. They claim that the science of Life and Immortality includes every department of man's nature- body, mind, soul, and spirit. Thus, every feature of daily living that is capable of affecting his welfare in any one of these departments comes within the legitimate domain of a full and satisfying philosophy or religion. Nor is a religion or a philosophy dishonored or lowered by being extended to include the practical aspects of man's four-fold being. In their emphasis upon these points, the Illuminati stand alone among schools of philosophy and metaphysics.

In regard to the doctrine of crucifixion of the flesh, adherents of the Temple of Illuminati encourage many items which are curtailed in the ordinary, strict religious body. On the other hand, they discourage and curtail many items that are regarded lightly by formal religious sects. Particularly is this true in applying the criteria of right and wrong to the domain of food and drink. Many a devoted worshiper would shudder at the very intimation of violating a single rule of ethics or morality, yet he may smile in derision at the mention of a philosophy that places discretion in regard to food and drink on a par with discretion in regard to moral conduct.

# THE WAY TO LIFE AND IMMORTALITY

Yet why should there be one law for man's moral nature and another for his physical being? The very law that bases right on the foundation of beneficence and profit, and that bases wrong on the foundation of harm and injury, in the domain of ethical culture and moral conduct, is the Law that obtains in like manner on the plane of physical welfare. The thought, word, desire, or deed that is productive of harm and injury either to the participant or to another is to be avoided. Thought, word, desire, or deed that is productive of positive good and helpfulness either to the participant or to another, provided it is free from harm to anyone, is to be encouraged. Similarly, food or drink which proves injurious to the physical being is to be avoided. No matter how pleasing it may be to the taste, if it retards physical functions and interferes with normal activity of the organs in any way, if it results in poisonous accretions, if it stimulates appetite to an abnormal degree, if it dulls or deadens or blunts the mental faculties- the food or the drink that leads to such conditions is to be avoided. The religious devotee to the laws of righteousness must learn to respect and to honor in his own life the laws of health and efficiency with as much devotion as he observes moral and ethical requirements. Likewise, the mystic, the seeker after truth, the aspirant after Mastership and Initiation, or the neophyte under training and guidance of a Master, must honor, the laws of health and efficiency with as much devotion as he observes the laws of prayer, sacred silence, and meditation. To the exoteric as to the esoteric he must pay his vows with equal reverence. The outer as well as the inner he must consult and obey. "As the outer, so the inner,"- in this as in all things else.

It is a principle not to be ignored that physical perfection, or the refinement and the purification of physical atoms, goes hand in hand with spiritual perfection, or perfection of soul. Thus, perfection of soul depends upon perfection of body. To indulge deliberately and willfully in habits that result in sorrow, sickness, misery, regret, and inefficiency is to be accounted a sin as grievous as violation of the law that says, "Thou shalt not kill." Harsh, radical, and cruel does it seem to claim that deliberate and willful harm or injury to the body, which weaken? it or shortens the earth life, is to be classed as one form of suicide. But the day is not far distant when the principle that identifies physical righteousness with moral righteousness will have become thoroughly established in the race consciousness. When that day has come man will honor spiritual law and natural law with equal veneration.

Another error in connection with law of crucifixion is the peculiar idea that in self-denial itself there is virtue, regardless of any legitimate reason for self-denial. Test of strength, proof of unselfishness, to deny oneself that which is particularly desirable! The greater the pleasure withheld, the greater the honor and the glory of being able to forfeit participation in it! Does the prodigal son manifest filial devotion by spurning the fatted calf, preferring still to live on husks fit only for swine? Such penance, such self-punishment, has no place in a rational religion. In the first place, it is unjust to oneself. In the second place, it is a dishonor to God.

In its final analysis, the Law of Crucifixion identifies itself with the Law of Justice, the Law of Balance and Equilibrium. It prohibits only that which is harmful. It encourages everything that is beneficent and helpful. It is by no means a hard and cruel master. Rather, it is generous and magnanimous in the extreme to him who honors and obeys its dictates in the spirit of humility and love.

The highest aspect, however, of crucifixion of the flesh is yet to be considered. Materially and spiritually, crucifixion has only one true meaning, namely, change, or transmutation. It is giving the life of the lower for the sake of the higher. It means that, through a correct system of living, on the three planes, mental and spiritual and physical, man must change body and mind from the carnal self into the purified being- a being that follows the doctrine of life, life still more abundant. The Law of Transmutation holds unflinchingly as its standard the aim that every thought and every act shall have as its ultimate purpose greater and more sublime life. This principle obtains on both the physical and the mental planes. To eat and to drink, to be clothed upon and to breathe the breath of life, to think and to plan and to cherish desires and ideals, to toil and to put forth effort- all is actuated by the one desire, the one motive, the one aim, even transmutation of the lower into the higher. Transmutation of dross into pure gold, of weakness into strength, of coarse and heavy vibrations into vibrations fine and light, of sluggish and inactive currents into currents alert and rapid; transmutation of material into spiritual, of imperfection into perfection, of irresoluteness into firmness of will-power; transmutation of selfishness into generosity, of malice and envy and bitterness into forgiveness and kindness and good-will, of ignorance and error and sin into knowledge and goodness and righteousness- this is the esoteric significance of the crucifixion.

The ordinary interpretation has emphasized the element of denial, or "giving up." To be sure, this element is necessary, for the lower must be given up for the sake of receiving the higher. The Illuminati, however, would paint the beauty and the grandeur of the higher, that which is to be received, rather than the pain and the anguish of separation from that which is to be parted with. In its true sense, denial means death. But the mistake of the ages has been in losing sight of the new birth that is to result from death or denial. Place emphasis on the glory of a new life, and the travail of birth is soon forgotten. Paint in lifelike colors the rose-tinted sunrise glow of the new morning, and the darkness of the darkest hour is lost to memory.

Remember, in the process of passing from the lower to the higher, from the carnal to the spiritual, there is death or denial or crucifixion only of the undesirable. The truly desirable is not to be crucified. There is no law natural or divine that calls for denial of that which is of permanent value. Many things in life, nevertheless, are of value only for the sake of being sacrificed.

The real value of many a so-called blessing consists in its ability to be transmuted into something of greater service. Silver coin is neither food nor drink, neither an ornament to the body nor a joy to the intellect. Yet it may readily be transformed into any or all of these. Likewise, according to the Law of Crucifixion, that upon which is passed the penalty of death is of value only by reason of its transmutability into something of intrinsic worth.

In this connection, let it be emphasized that normal, healthful pleasures are profitable to man as a means of stimulating higher forces. Consequently, self-denial in regard to them defeats the very purpose they are intended to serve. Miserly hoarding of money is self-denial in regard to expenditure; but it defeats the owner of the advantages to be gained by a judicious disposition of money. Likewise, strict, rigid self-discipline which refuses to satisfy normal, natural demands of body or mind may possess the virtue of self-control; but it fails to satisfy the Law of Transmutation. Normal gratification of normal desires for pleasure, whether physical, mental, or social, is of intrinsic value in that it stimulates to activity forces which would otherwise lie dormant and useless. The forces thus aroused may be directed into channels of usefulness, and thus serve a place of untold value. True self-denial in regard to innocent pleasures, therefore, consists in the attitude of mind one takes toward them. The correct attitude says: "I satisfy this desire not merely for the pleasure there is in it, but especially for the sake of stimulating forces and aspirations and ambitions which I intend to turn into channels of usefulness." This attitude of mind possesses the virtue of recognizing the Law of Transmutation. The lower motive of mere pleasure for its own sake is crucified. Rather, it is transmuted into, or gives its life to, the higher motive of receiving power and strength and stimulus to be directed into channels of lofty endeavor. On this principle, that legitimate joys and pleasures of both mind and body are not only permissible but valuable and even necessary to the highest culture, the Temple of Illuminati places great emphasis.

It is true that things in themselves desirable, as, pleasures and joys, which are the means of awakening dormant forces and potencies in one's life, serve as a medium of transmutation. It is true that normal gratification of these satisfy the Law of Crucifixion of the flesh when the lower motive is sacrificed to the higher. But, let it not be forgotten that there are many undesirable traits and qualities which must be overcome. The sacrifice or the transmutation of these is another form of satisfying the law of crucifixion. There are many desires and tendencies which must not be gratified. The self-denial that foregoes such gratification is one form of crucifixion. There are many habits thoroughly established in one's nature which must be corrected. The self-denial that rectifies harmful habits is another feature of crucifixion.

Chief among undesirable habits is the habit of destructive thought and feeling. Man must overcome and rectify this habit. He must change, he must transmute, undesirable thought tendencies into desirable. This is a denial, a sacrifice, a crucifixion, that demands painful execution. But he who holds to the ideal standard of healthful, constructive thought habits will count surrender as nothing in comparison with the gain to be derived therefrom.

Chief among destructive thought habits is the tendency to anger. This is a deadly passion which must be overcome. It poisons both mind and body. No good results from it. It is chief among deadly vices. No one truly desires to give way to anger, but the habit may gain such power over one as to seem uncontrollable. However, so long as there is life and a desire to overcome, there is hope. Let him who is a slave to this passion take courage. It is possible to transmute this habit into a power for good. The force that is now expended in the direction of anger and malice may be turned into the channel of good-will and wholesome service. The force or the power in an uncontrollable current of water is good. Gain control over it and put it to good service in running your machinery, and it is transformed from a danger and a menace into a benefactor. The force and the power manifested in anger is good.

Overcome the tendency, and change the current, and set it to work running your machinery according to the ideal of service to others; and you transmute its power into beneficence.

Overcoming the tendency to anger calls for great watchfulness and persistent effort. But the greater the price, the greater the reward. When the passion begins to manifest, immediately set to work to change it into good will and forgiveness and love. This demands extreme willpower and courage and persistence. This is a real crucifixion. It is difficult and painful, seeing that the passion is a part of one's very life.

Then there is the twin passion, jealousy. Of the vast multitudes, how many are free from this cruel passion? Rather, how few! How many are not in its grip? Rather, how few! Here is a mighty work to be accomplished. Here is a crucifixion that will be felt. Here is a powerful current the channel of which must be changed. Nevertheless, great is the reward of him who overcomes. Great is the price of victory. But glorious also is the crown of the victor. If it is a matter of jealousy because of possessions, one must control one's thought and wish another no less. He may, however, wish himself more, provided he puts forth legitimate effort to gain more. The force that might be wasted in grudges and jealousy must be turned into channels of honest endeavor to accomplish and to achieve.

In envy, also, there is opportunity for crucifixion. Within most people the passion of envy is very strong. It is difficult to understand why others, apparently not so worthy as we, apparently not laboring so hard as we, should have more than we. We forget that the soul has been eternally, and we know not what the soul of him whom we envy may have suffered. This passion we must crucify. We must change it into love. We must wish happiness for those whom we are tempted to envy. We must see that the crucifixion is complete and perfect. It is complete only when our desire for the welfare of others is a desire of the heart, sincere and true.

Thus, we see that crucifixion is real, that there is demand for it in the lives of all men and women. Crucifixion, however, is not a process of stifling, or stultifying, or destroying. This statement is true both in regard to natural, normal desires, passions, and appetites, whether of body, mind, or soul, which may be gratified, and in regard to undesirable traits and qualities and tendencies, which are to be overcome. Crucifixion is not a negative process. It is always a positive, active process. In the case of undesirable qualities, it is the act of changing them into desirable. In the case of innocent pleasures, it is the act of transmuting the thought of mere pleasure into the thought of awakening new forces to be used in channels of good. In either case, it calls for alertness and activity. The old idea of self-denial results in sluggishness and weakness of character. According to the teachings of the Illuminati, the Law of Crucifixion of the flesh results in power, strength, life- newness of life- life ever more and more abundant.

As we pass through these states of crucifixion, we gradually free the mind from bondage and from the fetters that hold it with rods of iron. Thus, freeing the mind from undesirable, destructive passions, we are at leisure to devote time to pursuits and interests that are pleasure-bringing and constructive. As these changes continue, the body becomes free from deadly poisons which have been generated previously by the deadly passions indulged in. As body and mind become free and strong, the soul becomes awakened and enlightened. Unfoldment and development of soul takes place. Gradually, mortality puts on immortality. Man becomes like the gods; and, in time, Sonship with the Father is established.

These are some of the principles underlying the doctrine of crucifixion of the flesh as taught by the Illuminati in Soul Science, the Way to Life and Immortality. They are not presented merely with the idea of satisfying an intellectual craving for speculation in regard to doctrinal points. They are for those who hunger after 'truth and righteousness, those who are desirous of living a life of usefulness and service, those who are anxious to apply to their own characters the measuring rod of self-discipline, aye, especially for those who are ready to honor and to obey the Law of Crucifixion as a means of transmuting dross and alloy into pure gold.

No amount of faith in Jesus as an extraordinary character, aye, not even faith in him as the only begotten Son of God and as one arisen from the dead, can suffice to redeem man from the bondage of ignorance, error, and sin. Faith, however, in the Law he made use of in order to demonstrate Sonship with the Father and power over death- this type of faith will work wonders in redeeming man from bondage to ignorance, error, and sin. Jesus was a deliverer in that he taught a doctrine and a system of living which will, when obeyed, deliver mankind from ignorance, error, and sin; from distress and wretchedness; from disease and death. An active faith in the Christ will lead to Life and Immortality.

## CHAPTER TEN

## LIFE WITHOUT RELIGION IS NOT HUMAN

Time and again it has been stated that religion is not necessary to the life of a people, that a people can attain the same height in culture, in enlightenment, and in all that makes life worth the living, without religion as with it. This doctrine, however, is false and even destructive.

Seemingly, this is an age of irreligion. Yet, underneath the surface, underneath the seeming truth, there is in the hearts of men, lying dormant perhaps, a religious current as strong as has ever been found in the hearts of men in any age. It is true that men have lost respect for the present form of religion, they have lost faith in current interpretation of truth. They have lost faith in the established church, in the vehicle through which religion is carried to the people. But we must not forget that the form is not religion, but only the vessel in which religion exists. Thus, the statement that men have lost faith in religion can not be substantiated.

Religion is life itself; and, without religion, there is no life. Religion is the link that connects man with the higher spheres. If this link were broken man would be nothing more than animal. He would not even be a savage; for the savage, though illiterate and uncultured, has a religion that covers every department of life.

There are men who claim to have no faith, who say that they believe in nothing. But watch a man that makes such a claim, watch him as he goes without his duties, watch him as he deals with men. Question him, and we find that his religion is a work, a method of business. He deals honestly with all men in all transactions. There is no outer restraint to compel him to follow methods of honesty. Ask him why, and you receive the answer that he thinks it is best. But, since there is no external restraint, why not indulge in dishonesty and accrue power and influence as well as money and possessions through selfish and illegitimate means? The same answer meets this question, "No, honesty is best." It may be unknowingly to himself, yet honesty to him is a religion; and he lives his religion faithfully. Nor is religious feeling dead within him. It simply does not express Itself as such be- cause he has not found a satisfactory means of expression. It is quietly awaiting the time when it shall have found a natural spontaneous avenue of expression. Say what we will, theorize as we may, religion is the only reality there is. Religion is not merely a belief, nor is it a mere faith. Religion is life itself. It is founded on the principle of life. It is, in fact, the principle of life; for it is the incentive back of life- the incentive that has called man into being. It is the connecting link between man and God. Were man able to free himself actually from this bond of connection, he would degenerate into a brute.

In proportion as man has this religious life within him, in that proportion will be his love for all that is worth while in life. Prayer and devotion to formal church worship are not the only ways by which man expresses religious feeling. The most frequent and the most nearly universal expression of religious sentiment is in love of the beautiful and the perfect. Love of flowers, of music, of art, of architecture, of symmetry and proportion- these are evidences of deep religious devotion. In fact, religion may be aptly defined as love for all that is beautiful. But beauty is the natural result of perfection and is proportionate to it. Therefore, it is equally true that religion is love for the perfect.. Proportionate to the religious life and the religious sentiment in one's nature will be one's devotion to the various expressions of beauty and perfection.

It is a fact patent to all close observers that men who are the most truly religious are the greatest lovers of music, of flowers, of art, of the aesthetic in all departments of life. It must be understood that fondness for the beautiful need not necessarily lead one away from the practical and the useful. For utility and true beauty go hand in hand. Beauty is only another name for perfection. The beautiful animal is a perfect specimen of its kind. The beautiful flower is a perfect sample of its class. Beauty in the equipments of a building is inseparable from the purpose it is intended to serve. The beautiful character is a perfect example of graces and virtues. The beautiful body is a perfect picture of health as well as a dream of pleasing tints and outlines. In fact, health is the secret of beauty in feature and in form.

In reality, beauty and perfection are synonymous terms. More than this, in the final analysis, religious sentiment and love of the beautiful and the perfect are synonymous terms.

Beyond all contradiction, religion has only one aim- that is, to perfect man. This is the one aim of religion in the present age. This has always been its aim, and always will be. Religion is not a formal faith, but a feeling; not a formulated belief, but a desire for perfection. It is faith in the beautiful and the perfect wherever found. it is belief in the ideal and in ultimate good wherever manifest. Its highest expression is in love for perfection of manhood and womanhood. Love for perfection as the goal placed before man and woman, this is evidence of religious life. Faith in the possibility of perfection is evidence of religious devotion. A purpose and a will-power that hold one to the ideal of perfection in every department of life, this is evidence of religious power and fervor.

It is a mistaken idea that religion is dead in the present age. The idea that men are irreligious at heart is a grievous misconception. At no time in the history of the world have men cared more for the harmonious and the beautiful as expressions of perfect development than in the present age. Evidence of this is seen in the tendency of. the age toward perfection in the various arts and trades, crafts and professions. Perfection of machinery claims the undivided attention of many a man. Many another man is devoted to the one purpose of reaching perfection in the cultivation of plant, or fruit, or flower. Perfect development of fowls and animals covers a large field in which the interest of many, is engrossed.

In the trades and in business activities, this spirit presents the appearance of rivalry and competition. Yet competition serves as a goad that stimulates one on to more skillful execution. Rivalry is a stimulus toward accuracy and delicacy- one form of perfection. The general demand for superior goods and superiority of workmanship incites a genuine love for perfect quality and for unquestioned skill in the preparation of products. Even the struggle for existence stimulates latent forces and unrecognized abilities in the expression of artistic tendencies. It must be admitted that economic conditions are by no means ideal and that rivalry and competition do not grow out of altruistic motives. Nevertheless, in spite of unjust conditions and cruel measures, religious life throbs under the tattered garb of many a humble workman who honors the ideal of doing his best in every undertaking. Many a lad, having the instinct of the beautiful, forced by poverty to a life of toil, finds satisfaction in giving artistic expression and perfect execution to the task at hand. His daily task may be a commonplace duty and implements may be crude; but he honors both the task and the implements by using delicacy of taste and accuracy of skill in execution. In this, he satisfies a deep-seated religious instinct, although he may consider himself an unbeliever and an agnostic.

It is an age in which love of the beautiful and love of harmony are made practical and useful. It is no longer considered that a lover of the beautiful is one who sits with folded hands dreaming of heavenly chants and ethereal color-effects. He is one whom nothing satisfies except the actual creation or expression of the beauty he feels. If circumstances debar him from finding an outlet for his artistic tendencies in the channel of his choice, he applies his love of harmony and symmetry to the task at hand. Nor is this all. Through faithful performance of commonplace duties according to a lofty ideal, in time, he makes for himself an opening in the line of his choice. Eventually, he becomes master of his art, and gives expression to the dream of his childhood.

It is true that men do not give expression to religious feeling in the same way they once did. Long, tiresome lip prayers fail to satisfy. Sermons the length of which is measured by hours are losing their power over men. It is true, however, that those who find religious form and ceremony irksome are generous in expressing their appreciation of the beautiful and the perfect wherever found. They are unrestrained in their praise of inspiring, soul-stirring music and art. Nor is praise given with insincerity and merely for effect. They are held enraptured by the power of harmony and rhythm in sound and in color and in movement. By this means they are enabled to forget themselves and to lose sight of concerns and interests which daily tax and harrow men's souls. This to them is worship. For this they give sincere praise.

The religion of the people is taking practical turns, and demands practical expression. This is an encouraging sign. Men are becoming lovers of the perfect in every department of life. Great is the mystery indicated by tills fact. Love of the perfect, in time, will cause men to seek perfection for themselves. Herein we read the signs of the times, the signs of the perfect state of man, which is to be when religion shall have become truly a life- a life that aims at perfection of body, mind, and soul.

For this reason do the Illuminati encourage men to seek the beautiful, and to love perfection for its own sake, and to surround themselves with the best and the highest art. We may not be able to lead men at one bound to accept the highest and the ultimate aim of religion- perfection and deification of manhood and womanhood. But, by giving men the best expressions of art and nature, we stimulate in them forces which tend eventually toward the ideal of a perfect race. The more the individual is encouraged in the gratification of that type of perfection which he most loves, the more quickly will he respond to appeals for perfection of character. Gratification of love for the beautiful in any line whatever is a stepping-stone toward love of perfection in human life. To argue that love for the beauties of nature is not a type of religious fervor is to argue that the letter A, is not a part of the alphabet.

Love for perfection and a desire to express perfection is the attracting center to which all men are being drawn. Believe it or not, men are becoming the points of steel, which are yielding, gradually but surely, to the attracting center.

And know this: God Himself is revealed to mankind through the beautiful and the perfect. The more nearly perfect an object is, the nearer it is to God and the more closely it resembles God. One epithet applied to God is Perfection. Love of the beautiful and the perfect in the heart of anyone gives evidence that there is in that heart a desire for God and for all that pertains to Him, The desire indicates religious life. It is the very life of him who is actuated by its fervor. Find a man who cares not for music, who takes no interest in things beautiful, whose heart is not stirred by tokens of perfection, and you have also found the man who cares not for life. He is the man who has no religion. Religions life has ebbed away and has breathed its last. He is no longer man in reality, but a broken reed shaken and tossed and blazon here and there by the wind, whether it comes from north or south, from east or west.

Love for the beautiful and the perfect gradually awakens in man a something of which he was heretofore unaware. This something manifests itself in a desire to be more worthy of all that is beautiful, a desire to be more ill harmony with it, a desire to be part of it. The awakening of these desires, in the beginning, will cause a restlessness, an indescribable longing, a hunger of heart, a yearning, a seeking for that which satisfies. In some manner, than should be led at this stage in his growth to see that everything for which he longs- all beauty and all perfection, all symmetry and all harmony, even all that is- is within himself. If the way whereby this is to be realized can be pointed out to him, all is well. For this desire will gradually become a Fire. Love of the beautiful and the perfect results in the desire to become perfect. For only in perfection of the self- body, mind, and soul- can one's love for beauty and perfection ever be fully satisfied. The desire for perfection becomes a Flame, which results ultimately in Illumination. Then it is seen how love of the beautiful and the perfect constitutes religion the most sincere and the most devout. Though it may manifest first as a passion for music and harmony or for the beauties of nature, in the end it becomes a passion for perfection of self- a burning desire to become like God. Mankind has been passing through stages of growth, which have led them to the place from which real progress will be made. The turning point has been reached; and definite progress is to be noted. Already progress is pointed out clearly in the history of the people.

Only a few centuries ago, men lived in self-denial, not in regard to things in which it is well to exercise self-control; but they went to the extreme of suppressing all expression of love for the beautiful. It was forbidden to be surrounded with objects of beauty. Many harbored the belief that music should be discouraged, that laughter is harmful. Asceticism, rather than religion, prevailed. Denial and repression originated in regard for a creed rather than in love for an ideal. In the hearts of men there was not so much love, not so much joy and peace, as in the hearts of those who today profess no religion, no church connection, but who are surrounded by objects of beauty and who cherish lofty ideals and generous thoughts. Many today who are classed as irreligious and non-believers in respect to outer forms of worship have in their hearts less hatred, jealousy, envy, and ill-will than did those of former years who made loud profession of faith. This is seen in the fact that in the early days of our history religious zeal led men to persecute and even to burn those whom they looked upon as witches. Thus, it is evident that, although men of our times do not make public profession of faith, and consequently are considered less religious, they are, in fact, more truly religious in that they are not so much in bondage to destructive passions and in that fellowship has a place in their hearts.

While progress is marked, yet this is only the awakening stage in the growth of the race. Soon will come the active developing stage, in which men will seek to find that which will give them life more nearly perfect and a more nearly perfect expression of life. Then men will live the life of development, the life that seeks conscious connection with the Godhead, and Illumination of Soul.

True, men have fallen from their divine estate; but this is not to say that they need to remain fallen. Rather, having knowledge of the fallen state, and knowledge of all states since the fall; and knowing that even the present life is far preferable to any of the stages previously passed, with this knowledge man is prepared to press forward, to go onward and upward, until the perfect state is reached. In the perfect state he will be as one of the gods, knowing good from evil, choosing the good because he realizes that only in the good is life to be found, and because he realizes that from evil death results. What was the prevailing doctrine of the age that we have just left behind? Was it that man should be perfect? Or was it rather that he should subscribe to a form and that outside of this form there could be no eternity? True, it was taught that man should obey God or be condemned. But how was he to obey him? In becoming perfect in body and in soul? Or, in crucifying the flesh, destroying it, and suppressing and stifling its normal demands?

What is the doctrine of the new age, the age just beginning?

"That man should redeem the body and cleanse the heart." This is the foundation upon which the religion, the very life, of the new age must be built. Not to crucify the flesh, not to ignore it, not to mortify the body, but to take care of it, to develop it, to cleanse it through right living and right thinking; to perfect the body so that it may become a beautiful temple in which the soul may manifest and become the Son of God- this is the doctrine of the new age.

The doctrine of the new age, the teaching of the Illuminati, is twofold. It teaches not only the upbuilding, the perfecting, and the beautifying of the body but also the cleansing of the heart. Man must free himself of all that is destructive in thought and thus build the Immortal Soul, the Soul that is redeemed and made whole. This is the basis of religion for the new age. It is a practical religion, a religion sanctified by God. It is a redemptive religion. This we know because those who have obeyed its teachings have found it practical and redemptive. Its principles can be applied to the every-day needs of life and the reward is manifold; but for those who accept it merely as an article of faith without living according to its requirements, there is no reward.

"Redeem the body that is thine, but also cleanse the heart that is within the body." This is the message that the Illuminati bring to all men. It is not mysterious and hard to understand, but it is a practical message full of life and inspiration.

## CHAPTER ELEVEN

## MAN, THE TEMPLE OF THE LIVING GOD

The great Law of Being always has been and always will be, as first expressed by the Thrice Wise Philosopher Hermes: "As it is below, so is it above." From this expression of the Law must all things be considered.

What do we think of a building in most respects perfect, which has here and there a blemish or a spot crumbling away in decay? The perfect lines, the superior style of architecture, and the faultless design are lost to view by reason of the few defects. Yet imperfection is the first to attract attention. The imperfect in the presence of the perfect is conspicuous by virtue of contrast.

Such a temple is the body of man. Man was created in the image of the Creator and himself endowed with the attributes of the Creator. Believe and think as he will, it is none the less true that the body of man is the temple of the living God. As such, it is an exact prototype of the beautiful temple structure in which men worship the Father. Although the body, temple of God, may be perfect in its construction and in its appointments, yet if it is marred through the effects of disease it is not a perfect temple. And worship therein- that is, the expression of God therein- can not be perfect so long as disease holds sway.

This fact brings us face to face with a serious problem, a problem that affects every living being. It is this; only one thing can fully manifest itself through the body at a time. Thus, the presence of disease in a body is conclusive evidence that God, the Divine Being, is not fully in possession of that temple, but that the carnal nature- call it what you will- holds sway. One nature or the other is master. One or the other predominates. God- that is, health, beauty, and harmony- prevails or evil- that is, disease, inharmony, suffering-, and sin- prevails. All that is perfect is of God. Nor is it altogether incorrect to say that all that is imperfect is of evil.

Without doubt, man is the temple of the living God. But it must be acknowledged that the temple may not be occupied by the living God. It rests with man so to prepare the temple that the living God will dwell therein. For it is an undeniable fact that the Infinite will not dwell therein unless the temple is a habitation fit for the Infinite.

This calls for a consideration of the concept, "Divine Being," or "the Infinite." Many do not think of the Infinite as a personal being, and are therefore skeptical concerning man as the temple of the living God. Each one is flee to lay aside every idea of personality and individuality in connection with Deity. One may even refuse to believe that there is a God. Yet the fact remains that if we do not give proper attention to the body, if we do not satisfy its normal requirements in regard to food, clothing, sleep, exercise, and other requisites of health and right living, there will be disease, which results in suffering, inharmony, distress, and inefficiency; consequently, we say that God does not dwell there. What matters it whether we say, God does not dwell in the temple or whether we say that health, happiness, harmony, love and forgiveness, and freedom from suffering do not dwell there? What matters it whether we say that God does not dwell there or whether we say that Perfection does not dwell there?

Men of the Illuminati believe in God. Yet, instead of limiting Him to definite boundaries of time and space, of personality and individuality, they think of the Infinite as including all things. He is health. He is happiness. lie is love. He is freedom from ignorance, error, and sin. Consequently, to say that disease, inharmony, ignorance, error, and sin prevail in a temple of flesh is equivalent to saying that God dwells not there, that Godhood does not predominate there.

# THE WAY TO LIFE AND IMMORTALITY

Think of a beautiful temple with perfection stamped on every feature, perfect in design, in architecture, in material, in decorations, and in appointments. Yet what is such a temple worth without a Godlike priest and without humble, sincere worshipers? Sad as it may seem, this corresponds exactly to a state of affairs that is to be guarded against in human life. It is possible for the temple of flesh to be apparently perfect in every feature and yet be desolate and unoccupied so far as Godhood is concerned. It is possible for the body to be a beautiful structure, a specimen of physical beauty and of physical perfection, and yet the character dwelling within may be destitute of divine attributes. It is possible for man to be perfect as an animal, yet be altogether carnal, altogether a temple of flesh. To be a perfect animal, to be a beautiful temple of flesh, is truly desirable, and is by no means to be discouraged. But this in itself is by no means all of life. This is not the divine plan and purpose for man. The divine purpose is that he shall be perfect man and perfect god. The possibility of becoming a perfect animal, destitute of active divine attributes; the possibility of his becoming a beautiful temple of flesh destitute of divine priesthood and divine rulership- this is a danger to be watched.

In building the perfect temple, man must have in view two things. In the first place, he must have in view the perfection of the body- a body perfectly healthy and normal, one that is free from disease and free from the suffering attendant upon disease. In the second place, he must have in view at all times the ideal of a strong and beautiful soul as the occupant and the ruler of the body. These two ideals must go hand in hand, perfection of body and perfection of soul. These two processes of development must go on simultaneously. The ideal is that when the body has reached a certain stage of development the soul shall also have become developed, illumined, and Godlike. Then man can rest assured that God dwells there. Then man will know that his body has become the temple of the living God. If man holds these two ideals constantly in view, every cell of the physical being becomes charged with this divine desire; and the body will not only be of healthy, normal flesh but will be flesh of His flesh, and the soul will be soul of His soul.

This twofold process is normal, healthful temple-building. This process changes mortal into immortal. It is not a process of destruction, or tearing down, but a natural process of building or changing, the natural process of growth.

When man has accomplished this great work; when, through his thoughts and his desires and through his habits of living, he has changed the body from disease and suffering to health and harmony; when the mind has become awakened, and the soul enlightened and illumined- then has God in very truth come to that man and has taken possession of the temple, and the man not only has become the Son of God but has attained the consciousness of being the Son of God. When man has become the temple of the living God, he will no longer think of a far-off heaven nor of the far-off event of entering into a distant heaven; but he will have already entered heaven, and will know that this life is a part of the greater life, and that it is in the Now that he enters into his heritage and becomes one with those great beings who have gone before. Heaven is where we make it, and what we make it. When heaven comes, or when one enters heaven, rests entirely with the individual. At the moment we shall free ourselves from bondage to those things which we do not desire, at that moment we begin to live the true life, and at that moment will the new life, the heavenly life, begin for us. The consciousness of life on a higher plane is heaven. The consciousness of harmony and peace, the consciousness of loyalty to a noble ideal, in whatever degree developed, whether in its infancy or in its maturity, is heaven to that extent. There are degrees of heaven as there are degrees of consciousness and of realization.

Life is a continual building. It took King Solomon all his life to build the great temple. In that building every bit of material was inspected so as to insure that it was perfect. So should we inspect every part of the material that is to become a part of our temple. We must see to it that nothing except, perfect cells are allowed to become part of the body. This calls for constant watching. Our thoughts and feelings must be carefully guarded and controlled. Thoughts and feelings of hatred, anger, ill-will must not be granted a place in our minds and hearts. Cells charged with hatred are no more fit to enter the bodily structure than are imperfect stones fit to be built into the walls of a temple that is to endure for ages.

If, in packing a barrel of fine apples with the idea of keeping them for a great length of time, one apple that is decayed should be left among the good, this one decayed apple would inoculate all the others around it, and in time the entire barrel of apples would be infected. So is it with the cells of the body. One cell charged with the vibration of anger will poison neighboring cells and will affect cells apparently healthy. Cells of hatred and anger are destructive in their effects, and consequently tear down rather than build up the physical organism. Thus a continual work of destruction goes on in the body of man. Besides the passions of anger and hatred there are many others, such as jealousy, envy, and kindred passions, which charge the cells with destructive, poisonous vibrations. This results in a diseased, abnormal condition in that part of the body in which the corrupt cells gain entrance.

When we understand this Law of Temple Building, when we bear in mind that every moment in the life of man is a moment of building, that not a moment passes without giving its share in the work of construction, that not food alone enters the body but that every thought, every desire, every passion enters the body and becomes the means of charging the physical cells with its particular type of vibration- then will we have the Key to life, health, and happiness.

# THE WAY TO LIFE AND IMMORTALITY

It must be emphasized in this connection that in this fact the Illuminati find the secret by means of which their healers are enabled to free man from disease. This mystery, this great truth, this law, the healer teaches his patient. He teaches the sufferer how to free his mind from passions and thoughts and desires which charge the cells with disease-creating vibrations. He teaches him how to substitute in their place health-creating vibrations- constructive thoughts, desires, and passions, which will charge the cells with health and with the truth that life is real and eternal to him who makes it so. It is utterly impossible for the man who thinks only of the good, the true, and the beautiful, who holds only thoughts of love, good-fellowship, and life to have a diseased body; for the cells that he is constantly building into the body are charged with these life-giving vibrations.

The principles here propagated picture the ideal state. But be it known that we can have just as much of the ideal state as we put forth effort to have. In proportion as we free the mind of hatred, anger, jealousy, and envy; in proportion as we hold thoughts of good-will, fellowship and love, in that proportion will we have health and peace and harmony, happiness and contentment. Results will be in exact proportion with the effort. If we free the mind and the heart altogether of destructive thoughts and desires, and if we eat life-giving foods, and observe other hygienic habits, near indeed will we be to perfection. The choice is ours. The work is ours. It is only a question of how much we desire these things and of how much effort we are wining to put forth to obtain them.

Another Item enters into this great work- that is, the elimination of the element of fear. No man can reach the highest so long as he allows fear to be a part of his nature. Fear is a great detriment to the attainment of perfection as are the deadly passions, anger, jealousy, envy, and malice. This is to be accounted for in the fact that fear prevents him from letting go of the old destructive life, and from taking hold of the new and greater, the constructive, life. Man fears this and that and the other. He fears that by letting go of the old life his neighbors and friends will talk about him or shun him. He fears that he may be deprived of pleasures which he now enjoys, that he may be required to sacrifice profits otherwise his. He forgets that by taking up the new life he will win friends and associates which will be of greater value to him than the old life afforded. He forgets that in the new life new pleasures will come, pleasures far more intense than were the old ones, pleasures which are not attended or followed by unhappy results as were the old. He will learn that true pleasures are constructive and healthful, and free from bitter after-effects.

Fear is the shackle that binds the millions to a life of misery, a life of suffering, a life that is in the main undesirable, a life that gives an hour of pleasure followed by months of pain and suffering.

Fear is the great black desert that Is to be found In the heart and the mind of the multitudes, a desert tract covering more territory than all else In the mind and the heart. Fear in the soul of man is like a swamp on a beautiful estate. Out of a hundred acres of land nine-tenths is profitless. If the swampy places, the low lands, are filled in and improved, there will be one hundred acres of beautiful, valuable land. If the swamp remains, there are only ten acres of valuable land; and even this is decreased in value by the unsightliness and by the miasma of the swamp. Thus is fear to man. It is covering and holding under subjection nine-tenths of his life. And even this one-tenth is overshadowed by the repressing influence of fear, and his efficiency is reduced by it.

If man can be made to see this fact; if he can be led to fill in this miasmic swamp of fear with thoughts and desires of the beautiful, of the lovable, and of the true; if he becomes interested in living in harmony with the Divine Law- then this swamp of fear is reclaimed, and man becomes a whole man. He will use all his faculties, which in time become free. Thus will man truly be the

Temple of the living God, Center of the measureless estate destined by divine right as his. He will become free from undesirable things, free from pain, free from suffering, free from disease and inharmony- the possessor of health, happiness, and Godhood, and of all that the consciousness of Godhood brings.

## CHAPTER TWELVE

### FEAR, THE GATE OF DEATH

Fear is a destroyer of power. It is the destroyer of life. Fear has held the vast multitudes back, has held them to believe only that which is believed by others, by friend, by neighbor, by instructor. Fear it is that draws the bands tighter and tighter until there is scarcely a breath of life left, by no means sufficient to maintain life as it should be maintained. Men have feared to do otherwise than believe that which had been taught them by those in authority. As a consequence, they were deluded into the belief that their own way of thinking must be abnormal and not to be trusted, that indeed thinking for themselves must be checked and given no encouragement whatever. Even the few who cherished ideas of their own feared to follow them as principles of life lest their ideas might be contrary to the teachings of recognized authority.

But now men are beginning to think for themselves. They are learning that each individual has a mind of his own for no other reason than to use in doing his own thinking. They are beginning to understand that the new cycle with its interpretation actually has for its foundation the principles of teachers and philosophers which men thought they had been following, whereas, in reality, they had accepted the teachers merely as external authority, and their teachings merely as a creed or a dogma with no adequate comprehension of their meaning. Men are beginning to realize that the value of teachings rests in the very fact of their being applied to the needs of daily life. To become convinced of the practical aspects of a philosophy or of a system of living, is to lead one to think for oneself. No one else can determine in detail the needs of an individual life, neither can external authority solve the problems that belong to the individual life. A great Master may interpret and expound general principles;

but each individual must study and think and contemplate for himself in order to have an intelligent comprehension of general principles in their adaptability to daily need. Of this fact men are becoming convinced. As a consequence, they are beginning to honor their own power of thought by trusting its conclusions.

The moment man begins truly to think, the moment he says to fear "Get thee behind me, Satan," at that moment will he really begin to live. For, with the thinking, will come newness of life, which will be an incentive for more independent thinking and an incentive to action, an incentive to dare, to do, and to live. Thinking, acting, and living in harmony with the Divine Law in time results in a new life, a life that is worth the living. This new life often brings a struggle because it is not entirely in harmony with the ideas of those around us; but, when the mind is fully awakened to the ideal of a new life, it is not easily led astray, but persists in following the path indicated by the Law.

Fear is not life. It is death. In reality, fear is hell. If there were no other deadly passions or vices to punish us, fear alone would be a hell terrible enough to satisfy the most orthodox. It is fear that prevents man from doing his best, fear to think, fear to act, fear to be an individual, fear to do this and to do that. To be under the thralldom of fear is a bondage, aye, even a bondage worse than the Hebrews are said to have suffered in ancient Egypt.

The Illuminati are teaching men to free themselves from the bondage of fear, to free themselves from all undesirable conditions, and to live as they think they should live, in spite of the opinions of men and in spite of authority-taught doctrines. They teach men to free themselves from every fear except one-fear of the Divine Law when they do contrary to the dictates of their own conscience. There is no true freedom in disobeying that which one knows to be right. This fear man must encourage. This is fear of God, fear to dishonor and to disobey Him. In this sense, fear of God is reverence and devotion.

# THE WAY TO LIFE AND IMMORTALITY

The incentive for man to overcome fear is twofold. First, there is the freedom from fear, which in itself is a great satisfaction. Second, there is the satisfaction of realizing that fear may be transmuted into power. Thus, the principle by which fear is overcome is both positive and negative. It insures freedom from an undesirable state; but, in addition to this, it insures a positive, active power to take the place of the undesirable state of fear. Fear is to be overcome through the Law of Transmutation. The power expended or wasted in fear is to be transmuted, or changed, into power for good, power to accomplish and to achieve. Every passion known to man, every chain and fetter that holds him, when changed, becomes just as great a power for good. For this reason, the Illuminati do not advocate destroying, or killing out, or stifling, any passion or tendency no matter how undesirable it may be. They teach men how to change the undesirable into desirable, how to turn the direction of power into desirable channels.

A hell of fire and brimstone finds no place in the teachings of the Illuminati. Hell as a place in which man is punished for things done that should not have been done, is not recognized by the Illuminati. That man is punished for his sins either here or in the hereafter is an erroneous idea. That he is punished by his sins here and now as well as in the hereafter is a truth that each individual ought to comprehend. Of those conditions which punish man, fear is one of the most terrible. The man who fears is in Hades, or hell, as surely as man ever can be. Who knows not the awful suffering caused by waiting for something to happen which one thinks is to happen? The fire, the suspense, the dread, the uncertainty- this is hell! Sitting and waiting, expecting something to happen, fearing to move, fearing to act, fearing to think, aye, even fearing to breathe- this is hell, destructive to soul and body alike!

But such conditions must pass away. Man must be- come the master. He must understand the promises made to him by the Divine Will. He must do more than understand them, he must believe and trust them. Not merely in a formal way but in a practical way must he trust them, manifesting his faith by acting as if he had faith in the promises of God. He must think, act, and live according to his faith in the Law. As he does this, it may be with shrinking in the beginning, he will gradually free himself from fear. Fear is a terrible nothing, which gives way as knowledge and understanding increase.

Fear can not be mastered by mere faith in a promise of God. It can be overcome only by living in harmony with the Divine Law upon which the promise rests. Fear as well as all other undesirable conditions give way only as we manifest faith in the Divine Law by living in harmony with it. For thus do we grow into love and wisdom and true understanding. In exact proportion as one grows in love and wisdom does fear vanish. "Perfect love casteth out fear."

Life throughout is a growth. All true knowledge is a growth. Mere belief in the truth of a statement does not constitute knowledge. Mere acceptance of the statements of another does not constitute knowledge. Knowledge is that which we feel within us, that which we realize to be a part of our very lives, that which we know because it is a part of our consciousness. The more we live in harmony with the Divine Law, the more true knowledge shall we receive. Knowledge is like a mustard seed. Accept a little and live accordingly, and it will bring us into more and more knowledge, and deliver us more and more from the bondage of fear and ignorance. Fear is the out-growth of ignorance and error. Courage, faith, and hope are the outgrowth of knowledge and love. All conditions under which man suffers have a work to perform, a mission to fulfill, a purpose to satisfy. Through them, man gains knowledge and wisdom. Without suffering, man could not know what freedom from suffering means. Without having known fear man could not understand or appreciate freedom from the bondage of fear. Without knowledge of hate, man could not realize the power and the beauty of love. Without experiencing the absence of love, little would he know of the potency and the efficacy of love. Thus with all the passions and vices and undesirable conditions. Man must know of them in order to choose their opposite. The only reason for knowing evil is to enable one to choose the good. Nor does this indicate that man must indulge in evil for the sake of appreciating the good, nor that he must deliberately experience wrong and error and sin and suffering for the sake of knowing the value of their opposite.

The work of man, now that he is on the earth plane, is to transmute all undesirable things, no matter v/hat they are, into desirable. This is true whether it concerns the destructive passions, hale, anger, malice, ill-will, or whether it concerns the deadly poison, fear, or whether it concerns any other undesirable habit to which our natures cling. They must all be changed into health, strength, harmony, wisdom, happiness, and finally and ultimately into Immortality. Also, thus is it with that which we now consider a task, a duty, a yoke, that which we carry not because we must but because we think we must. Even this may be transformed from a yoke of bondage into a garland of flowers, a yoke of love, a privilege, which we would not part with even if we could free ourselves from it.

Man must be bound to something. Otherwise, he would stand alone and separate from all else. But his is the choice of the bond. He may choose fear and the bondage that results from fear, leading ultimately to death. Or, he may choose love and all that comes with the divine passion love, leading ultimately to Life and Light and Immortality.

The very beginning of the true life, of all true knowledge, and even of the very end itself- Individual Immortality and Sonship with the Father- is at the moment man accepts the glorious truth that he is created in the image of the Father, the truth that in himself are all powers, all capabilities, all that is in God, the first Creator, though in less degree, in fact, the truth that man is the temple of the living God. But this is only the very beginning. This is the point from which he makes the start. Having accepted this truth, he must, like the builder of temples and mansions, learn the art of building from the very foundation up until the temple is finished. He must learn what material to accept, what material to refuse. He must learn how to direct the work, and how to continue faithfully until the building is complete and beautiful in its perfection.

When man accepts the first truth, the foundation principle, and begins to build according to his understanding of the truth, he will also begin to know what it means to be free, not only free from bondage but free from those other things which bind him through fear. As he begins to live, so will he begin to grow. As he grows, so will he manifest those fruits which are always the result of natural growth.

Man is not made to fear. Man is not made to suffer, surely not made to die. Man is made to be free, free and fearless as is his Creator. He is made to enjoy life, and to know happiness, He is made in the image of the Father, to live forever. And so shall he live forever when he has freed himself from fear, from limitations and from those race beliefs which now bind him to the enemy that leads to death.

`The soul seed that is now in man could not gain knowledge without the body, the flesh that is of the earth and earthly limitations; consequently, through its own volition, it fell into matter and into the shortcomings and limitations of matter. It is impossible for the soul again to know God and become like Him and to return to its ideal state, though retaining the knowledge it has gathered during the earth life, without accepting the great truth that the present life is not only for the purpose of gaining knowledge and understanding but more especially for the purpose of redeeming the soul from all undesirable conditions. The soul redeems itself not through some special favor granted It by God, but through its own efforts, through its own worthiness, and through its own desires and volition.

Redemption, full and complete and perfect, has reference not only to the soul but to the body as well. Final redemption means freedom of body and soul. The body shall become purified and freed from the elements that hold the carnal being. The body shall become partner and co-worker with the soul, sharing its pleasures, its joys, and its harmonious conditions with the soul, states which the soul can not enjoy alone.

To what desire in man can we point above all others to prove that death is not planned by the Divine Will as the goal for man? What desire, above all others, holds most men, and is the strongest in men? Search man, search all men, for the deepest desire of the heart, not merely for that which they claim to desire but for that which they actually desire in their hearts. There are those, numberless indeed, who, not having health, desire health. There are those, numberless also, who, not having love, desire love. There are those, multitudes of them, who, not having worldly possessions, desire possessions. And there are multitudes who desire other things. But these are not the great desire in the universal human heart. They are strong desires, it is true; but there is one greater, one stronger, a universal desire- that is, the desire for life.

According to the Masters and the Philosophers, it is actually possible for man to attain that which his heart desires, provided he is willing to make the effort, to give the self-denial and the struggle necessary to attainment. This being admitted, who is there to deny that the desire for life, being the strongest and being universal with a few exceptions, is therefore a desire capable of fulfillment? Especially must we grant this when we learn that every true teacher and philosopher, including the Master Jesus, promised the redemption of both soul and body.

# THE WAY TO LIFE AND IMMORTALITY

Eternal life will not come to man through a knowledge of eugenics merely and through obedience to the laws of race improvement. Nor will it come through perfection of body only, no matter how desirable that may be. Life eternal is possible only when men understand that it is necessary to perfect both body and soul at the same time; when they understand that with the desire for continued life they must also desire a perfected, a developed, an illumined, soul This twofold desire- the desire for perfection of both body and soul- must charge every cell, every atom, in the entire body. Thus every cell is charged with life, not only with physical life, so-called, but with spiritual, heavenly life as well.

This can be accomplished. It is only necessary for the human family to accept the promise, and, having accepted it, to live according to the teachings and the laws given with the promise. Think of life; but, while thinking, also live in harmony with the thoughts of life. Charge every cell of the body with the thought of life. Charge every cell of the body, not with fear, but with freedom; not with hate, but with love; not with grudges and ill-will but with forgiveness; not with envy of the possessions of others, but with blessings to them, blessings and the sincere wish that their blessings may bring them happiness and fuller life- with blessings to them and with the wish that you yourself may gain possessions, not theirs, but your own, to bring happiness and satisfaction.

Life is always life. It is in the living that we gain the results of living, no matter according to what doctrine we live, whether it be the doctrine of life or of death. God is the God of life; but He prevents no one from following the doctrine of death and of partaking thereof.

## CHAPTER THIRTEEN

## THE WRONG LIFE, THE LIFE OF SIN, ALONE BRINGS DEATH

What is sin?

On the answer to this question depends everything in so far as it has to do with a full life.

Not only is sin something which affects the soul and gives it its status in the life beyond death, but it is something which affects man here and now. Sin has been considered as a wrong committed which denies him entrance into the realm of bliss in the Hereafter. It has been considered as acts committed daily, perhaps hourly, including evil thoughts and evil deeds and wrong living, the only direct effect of which is to prevent man's entrance into a realm of delight and joy and peace. It has been considered as thoughts, desires, and acts which are contrary to the will of God. While it is true that these acts do affect the status of the soul in the Hereafter, and that they do affect its relation to God, by no means do their effects end here. That they affect the personality and the individuality, that they affect the health and strength and efficiency, that they affect the peace and the satisfaction and the harmony of life here and now is a truth that needs to gain a stronger hold on the race consciousness.

In Soul Science, the Illuminati teach and hold as an absolute fact that any thought, any desire, or any act, no matter what its nature, is a sin if in any way it is injurious either to the participant or to anyone else. On the other hand, they hold it not merely as an article of faith but as an actual truth that any thought, any desire, or any act which is not injurious to the participant and which does not bring suffering and sorrow to anyone else is neither a wrong nor is it a sin. From this, it is seen that there is no difference between what is called a sin and what is called wrong doing or wrong living or working against the interests of others. In principle, they are the same. From this, it appears that hygienic law is on an equality with moral and ethical law; that care of the body is as important as regard for the soul; that habits which concern the welfare of the physical being, whether in regard to food and drink or in regard to any other factor of health and efficiency, are to be classed as injurious or non- injurious, and consequently as right or wrong, as upright or sinful. To indulge in eating or in drinking that which is harmful to the physical being is not only a wrong to the person, but is actually committing a sin- a sin that affects the soul as well as harms the personality here and now. Sin is a death-bringing agency, a destructive principle, a harmful and injurious habit. To lead the wrong life- wrong merely in that it concerns the physical being- is living a sinful, a death-bringing, life.

In the earth life, the body is as important as the soul. Otherwise, God would not have given man a body. To entertain happy, wholesome, generous thoughts is not all of righteousness. The thoughts and the desires of an individual may be free from carnality and free from every form of selfishness, jealousy, envy, ill-will, in short his life may be apparently a model one; but, if he gives his entire attention to business or to the work at hand, if he does not give the physical being the attention it deserves, if he does not allow time for sleep and does not provide proper food so that the body is recuperated and nourished- then, it follows that he is guilty of violating physical laws and is consequently guilty of sin and error as truly as if he violated so-called moral law.

Moreover, God is a just God, which means that He is a God who balances all things; for only in the balance and ill perfect equilibrium of all things is there justice. It follows, therefore, that the body is no less important than the soul, nor is the soul greater than the body, since the soul's greatness depends in large degree on the perfection and the purity of the body, and the perfect, well-balanced soul can not dwell in an unclean body.

Thus, it follows that the wrong life is the sinful life, and the sinful life is the life that brings disease, sorrow, suffering, and, in the end, an ignoble death- death which was never intended by God, death which became a necessity only when man gave up the true rule of life and accepted the belief that death of the physical is necessary, thus charging and magnetizing the cells of the body with the thought of death and the necessity thereof.

God made man in His own image. That is, as God is sinless and ever living, knowing no death, so did he make man. But with perfection he gave man free-will, a faculty that He also possesses. Being perfect, God holds only perfect beliefs. He gave perfect beliefs to man; and man, as first made, was perfect. But he was not satisfied with simplicity and perfection. Consequently, he used the power, or the gift, of free-will for wrong purposes. Thus, did he gradually fall into those conditions, desires, and beliefs which made death a necessity. Having been made perfect, man should therefore be sinless, and as a natural consequence, he should be deathless.

The Illuminati regard it as a fundamental truth that man may gradually and naturally find the path that leads to sinless, sorrowless, deathless life. But, in order to do this, he must make two important changes. First, he must change his thoughts and his desires and his beliefs. He must entertain only thoughts and desires and beliefs which harmonize with the doctrine of a life that is free from illness, sorrow, and death. Second, he must change his life and conduct to coincide with the change made in thought and desire and belief. He must begin living the natural life, giving to his body the food and the drink, the recreation and the rest, which God intended it to have.

He must cease making business his supreme god, the god that claims all his thoughts and desires and all his time. He must live for the sake of living. He must not live merely because he wants to be successful in business and outdistance his competitors. He must not sacrifice pleasures, friends, family; and, last and greatest, he must not sacrifice his soul and his God for business as the multitudes are doing. But he must give each and all of these interests part of his time, as much as the Divine Law, the Natural Law, demands for his own welfare. There are those who will say that this is impossible. But proofs are at hand that man does sooner or later satisfy the Law in this respect. If he does not do it willingly, the Great Law demands it by taking him from his business through sickness, or through suffering, or through misfortune, and finally through an immature death.

The question then comes. What is man willing to do? Is he willing to apportion his time judiciously among the varied interests that should claim his attention? Is he willing to meet the normal demands of his nature for development of body, for recreation and pleasures? Is he willing to satisfy the demands of his soul and the voice of God speaking through his soul? Is he willing to live the natural, normal life, a life that is free from disease and suffering, a life that is long and happy, a life that achieves success on all planes of being? Or does he prefer to live the strenuous life, the life that has no time for physical development or temple-building or natural pleasures, no time for home and friends and God, a life that has time only for business and zealous competition?

With man is the choice. He can choose the sinless life- that is, the natural, normal life. Or he may choose the unnatural, death-bringing life. His is the choice. The principle that concerns man also concerns woman.

The same law that governs man also governs woman. In the case of woman, however, it is slavery of another kind, not thralldom under business demands, but slavery to unnecessary home cares, to dress, to society, and to hundreds of other concerns which seem necessary to womankind, but which are unnatural and abnormal. The interests to which woman becomes a slave she herself admits are not a source of true happiness. She follows them in the same spirit in which a man follows his business, simply because competitors are to be outdistanced.

Such subjects as these are not generally supposed to have any connection with a philosophy that concerns the soul and man's relation with God. They are, nevertheless, the very foundation of freedom from disease and suffering, and freedom from sorrow and unhappiness. They are the very foundation of a long and useful life, of soul development, and of Illumination, and finally of the attainment of heaven and Immortality. They are the foundation upon which the temple structure is to be erected. If the foundation upon which man builds is unsound, the whole structure will be insecure and will not bear the test of time.

Man is created in the image of God- that is, in the image of the Perfect. He bears the image, or the possibility, of perfection in respect to body and soul and spirit alike. Although this likeness to the Perfect is only in embryo, it is none the less a veritable possibility of perfection. Then why should man be sinful? Why should he do those things which ate conducive neither to perfection of body nor to perfection of mind and soul? And yet it is to be freely admitted that practically all men are living and thinking contrary to the Law of Perfection as it regards body and mind and soul.

Generally considered, man is a carnal, sinful being- a creature of wrong acting and wrong thinking, one who gets at naught both Natural and Divine Law. It is for this reason that he is punished. Not the anger of a just God but his own acts and his own thoughts are responsible for the punishment that he suffers. Not by God is he punished but by the thoughts and the acts and the desires of which he himself is guilty. When sickness, sorrow, and finally death come to him, he blames God, he blames Nature, he blames everything except himself- the very one that is indeed accountable for that which befalls him.

So much has been taught concerning the Divine Law and the laws of nature that man can not plead ignorance regarding them. Although many doctrines have been given a false representation, yet, if man followed them according to the best light he possesses, his condition would be far better than it is. Even if he followed prevalent teachings merely because he thought they concerned the soul in its future state he would even then be far better than he is at the present time.

But we are now reaching an age in which man must know not only that religion concerns the soul but that it is actually the Law of God covering every department of his nature. Or, if one does not claim to believe in God, let him understand that religion is the Law of Nature, and that it deals primarily with the well-being of the body and with all those things which really concern life in its first application to man. Let him understand also that in proportion as religion is applied to the life of man on the material plane so v/ill it have its effect on the soul plane.

Religion will come to be understood as the Law of Life. Life, in this sense, refers to existence as it is from the moment that the Divine Spark leaves the Creator, no matter who or what is thought of as the Creator, down through its birth, onward through life, and still onward until man enters the immortal Life. It matters not where life shall continue, whether on the present plane of being or in the Beyond in the soul realm, nevertheless, true religion is the Law of Life and includes everything that concerns man on every plane of his being.

God is not a sinful, nor a sorrowful, nor yet a dying God. God is Life. God is Light. God is Love. God is wisdom. God is Happiness. God is Eternity. Man is created in the image of Light, of Love, of Happiness, of Life Eternal. Man is heir to all of these things; but he can enter upon his inheritance only as he complies with the Divine Will which has existed since the very beginning of time. Unless he obeys the requirements of the Divine will in its true spirit rather than according to the letter, he can not inherit the benefits and the blessings that the Divine Will wishes to confer upon him. Thus, as God is an eternal reality, free from undesirable things, so can man be free from those conditions which none desire if he is willing to obey the Divine Law and lead the life that normal, natural, divine man should live.

As man now is, he may conclude that this means self-denial and the giving up of all those things which make life worth the living. But this is a false conclusion. True religion denies man none of the tidings that are good for him. It denies him no honest, wholesome recreation. It does not deny social intercourse nor does if forbid him an honest business or the following of an honorable profession. Neither music nor flowers nor the beauties of nature or of art are denied him. The true religion forbids nothing except that which is not good for one. It denies one only those pleasures, so-called, which bring no good but plenty of ill, those things which bring sorrow and pain and death. And who can say that these things are actually desirable and that they form a necessary part of life?

In the teachings of Soul Science, the Illuminati encourage everything that is for the well-being of man. They attempt to teach only those things which will help him to become a perfect being, one that lives right and believes right. They teach that perfect faith is necessary, and that it is necessary to live in harmony with perfect faith. This is the Way to Life and Immortality.

## CHAPTER FOURTEEN

## HEALING OF THE SICK, POSSIBLE

Those who have learned the truth either through experience in the world or through training receive a two-fold command from God. First, they are to teach the truth to the multitudes that do not yet know the truth. Second, they are responsible for heeding the divine command, "Heal the sick." Consequently, those who fulfill their full duty must teach and heal, teach and heal those who come to them in faith.

In this department of the great work- that concerning teaching the truth and concerning healing- little can be accomplished unless the teacher-healer demands faith in the possibility of healing and faith in its realization. This is not unnatural nor is it unreasonable. Moreover, we find that all teacher-healers, including the Master Jesus, demanded faith on the part of those who came to them for healing. Unless they had faith they could not be healed. This is not an arbitrary demand on the part of the teacher-healer. It is rather to be considered as a necessary condition of healing, a state of mind that makes it possible for the sufferer to receive or to appropriate healing power. In this sense only, is faith essential. The law of healing is expressed in the oft-repeated saying of Jesus, "According to thy faith so be it unto thee."

In healing the sick, something more is required on the part of the healer than use of healing power. It is absolutely necessary for the teacher-healer to teach the Divine law, the natural life, to those who come to him. Unless he does this, though he may heal them for the time being, the disease or some other disease will return; for that which caused disease in the first place will cause a recurrence of it.

# THE WAY TO LIFE AND IMMORTALITY

In Soul Science, the Illuminati hold it as an absolute fact that wrong living, or unnatural living, as regards food, drink, sleep, exercise and employment of mind and body, is a sin because it is in violation of divine and natural law. He who so sins will be afflicted sooner or later with some disease, no matter how great his faith may be, unless he lives in harmony with his faith and' puts his faith into practical effect. God desires man not only to have faith in His goodness but to live in harmony with the faith he possesses. The Illuminati hold that the sufferer's faith in the healer and in the power of God through the healer may be so great that disease which has afflicted the body for many years may fall away as though it has not existed. But they further hold that if his life in the future is not in accordance with natural law the body can not remain free from disease and suffering. This is the teaching of all true Masters, including Jesus.

That illness is in reality sin, or the result of sin, is amply indicated in the sayings of Jesus. In some instances, he said, "Be thou whole"- that is. Be thou free from disease. In others, he said, "Thy sins be forgiven thee." Yet again, "Go thy way and sin no more." This saying concerns the future of the one healed, and indicates clearly and undeniably that a recurrence to sin would result in a recurrence of the same disease or in some other difficulty. Consequently, the Illuminati maintain that the chief duty of the healer is to teach those whom they heal the laws of life, natural and normal methods of living, even the way of Life. It is as important for them to understand how to keep free from sin and disease and suffering as it is to be healed in the first place.

Yet again, the mission of the teacher-healer extends further even than this. Not only to the body does he minister, freeing it from its load of fear and suffering, but the heart of the sufferer he heals, the heart that is also heavily laden with sorrow caused by sin. The heart that is free from sin has no sorrow. It understands the things that come to it, and even the passing away of a loved one does not bring it the pain and the anguish that come to the heart that sins. The heart that is free knows that death is only a transition, that "passing away" is only temporary. The heart that is set free from sin does more than believe; for in belief there may be suffering: it knows, and in knowledge there is freedom.

Why should faith on the part of the sufferer be necessary if God is all-inclusive? Why should not the teacher-healer be able to charge and to magnetize the body of the afflicted with healing vibrations so as to free him from illness in spite of lack of faith?

In answer to this question, let it be understood that the Law ever has been and ever will be that a substance, no matter what its nature, cannot receive unless it is prepared to receive. Thus, in the making of a magnet, not every substance will receive the charge of electricity and retain a part of it and through its power become a magnet. Only certain substances can be charged and become magnets. All things are under natural law. The body of the sick is under natural law. Though charge upon charge of healing power might be sent through the diseased body, health will not be brought to it unless the body has been prepared to receive and to retain the healing power. Now, faith is the agency that prepares the body to receive and to retain healing power. If the afflicted one has not faith in the healer and in healing power, he is like the piece of metal that is unprepared for the electric charge. The charge is received by the metal; but, instead of being retained, it goes right through the metal, and nothing is accomplished.

The greater the faith, the greater will be the result. If faith is strong and unwavering, the healing power, on being received, will so charge and magnetize every cell of the body that the vibration of health, being higher and more intense than the vibration of disease, will literally burn out the diseased condition and will charge and magnetize the cells of the body with health. Thus those who were suffering will be made whole. Thus sins will be forgiven. Such is the promise.

From this, it is to be seen that the law is, "According to thy faith, so shall it be unto thee." There is no power on earth, none in heaven, none under the earth or in the sea, which can heal the afflicted body and mind if there is not faith, faith that shall receive and retain the healing power as it flows from the fountain of life- directly from the Godhead, the Great Storehouse of Light and Life and Love, through the teacher-healer to the suffering one.

The old theory that it is God, or the Lord, or Jesus, who performs the work of healing is denied by the Illuminati. To be sure, the healing power comes from God; but He is not the healer in an arbitrary sense any more than He is the one who commits the sins that cause the diseases. Man who thinks wrong and lives wrong- he it is who, through wrong thinking and wrong living, brings disease and suffering and sorrow upon himself. Likewise, through right thinking and right living and through faith in health, man will draw to himself and will retain the vibrations and the power that shall overcome disease and suffering and sorrow, and that shall restore health. True it is that the healing power belongs to God. But it is by no means correct to say that God gives it. Rather, He allows man to take it. He permits man to receive and to use it. Man is not a slave, he is free. Man is not the supplicator of God, he is a partaker with God. Man is free to use, to receive, as he will.

God has made man in His own image. He has also created a storehouse of life, of force, of energy. To man he has given the key to this Universal Storehouse. This key man is free to use according to his need. The key is faith and life. He who has faith and he who will live, is enabled to draw from this storehouse as much as he can use. The more he uses, the more he can draw therefrom. Neither does God give to him nor does He deny him. Man is free to accept and he is free to use.

There are conditions, however, to the acceptance and the use of these powers and energies. The first condition is faith. The second condition is that man shall live according to his faith. If he does not meet these two conditions, he loses the key to the Storehouse and can not draw therefrom. God does not force us to accept, but He gives us the privilege to draw on the Storehouse of the All Good. If we have lost the key, the power to draw therefrom, and are in need, it is often necessary for some one to act as intermediary, as agent between us and the Father. It is then that we have need of the true teacher-healer. Such service Jesus and the other Masters gave to mankind.

The Illuminati maintain that God punishes no man, and that He sends neither sorrow nor misery nor sickness nor misfortune to anyone, but that man through his own thoughts and acts draws to himself the conditions that befall him. Not for his sins but by his sins is man punished. The Law operates both ways. As he draws undesirable conditions, disease, suffering, and misfortune through his manner of thought and his manner of life, so may he draw to himself the things that are desirable, such as Life, Light, Love, and Immortality. Instead of thinking, desiring, and living the life that leads to death, he begins to think, desire, and to live the life that leads to Life Eternal, and "all things are added unto him." Through his changed manner of thought, of feeling, of life, he draws to himself not disease, not sorrow, not death, but Life and light and Love. God gives neither the one nor the other. He merely permits man to draw from the Storehouse and to use. God denies man nothing, neither good nor bad.

He gives man the privilege to do as he pleases and to bear the result of his doing.

In a very true sense, it is not God who restores the sick and the suffering. Faith and living according to faith- this it is which restores to health the sick and the suffering. Nor is it God who takes life. Nor is it He who sets the time of death, nor is it He who numbers the days of man's life. He gives man the privilege of living, and of obeying the Law, and of living in accordance with the Law. Clearly does He indicate that to him who fully obeys there shall be neither sickness nor death. But He gives man no reason to believe that God, the Father, will overcome death for man. Lie makes the truth unmistakably clear that man must overcome death for himself. This he must do not by faith alone, but by works according to faith, and by living the life that knows no death.

The past cycle, the past age, has believed and has taught to suffering humanity that redemption, salvation, immortality do not concern the body. No matter how pain-racked the body might be, no matter how diseased, no matter how great its suffering, if man has faith in salvation, faith that at death the soul will fly to heaven-humanity has been taught that with such a faith as this salvation would be complete. But that age is ended. Men now know, even those who do not believe in religion, that salvation is not of the soul alone, but that it concerns the body as well. They know that the body is only the reflector of the soul. They know that the soul within, when it has reached Illumination and enlightenment, will illumine the whole body. They know that as is the God within, so will become the body without; and, in like manner, as is the body, so must be the soul, because the body when made perfect is the temple of the living God.

But we must not overlook the fact that the body may be perfect in appearance, that it may be healthy as a body, and yet be destitute of goodness, destitute of soul. For there are animal natures in the form of mankind wherein is neither goodness nor soul. These can scarcely be classed as human beings. They are healthy and of good form like the animal that is well fed and well tended. Furthermore, they resemble the animal in that their thoughts, like the instinct of the animal, make no impression upon them. Like the animal, they are pawns in life's great being. They come and they go. They live and they pass on. But, says the critic, How can this be consistent with the teaching that every thought, every desire, every act, makes an impression upon the body and produces corresponding effects?

True indeed it is that thought, desire, and act leave the impress of their character upon the body and affect the body accordingly. This is a Law not to be ignored. But there is another Great Law, a Law not generally known. To illustrate; a dog may be perfect in every respect, yet be possessed of a vicious temper, a temper that makes the dog dangerous, so that it is not safe to give him freedom lest he injure those who come near. The vicious nature of the dog does not shorten his life, nor does it interfere with digestion of food, nor does it impair the health of the dog. Why not? Simply because it is the nature of the dog, and he lives according to his nature. Had the dog a soul, a something in his being which gives him the right and the power of choice, then viciousness would act as a poison to his system and would result in disease and suffering; but the dog has not a soul. Consequently, he is born, lives, and dies, what he is, merely a vicious dog.

Hard as it may seem, there are those born in human form who are like the dog in nature. Through some cause, but always of their own choice, they have destroyed the individuality within. They no longer possess that something, called the Divine Spark, which makes them responsible for their acts. They simply live the life of their nature, There is nothing within to receive and to reflect their acts and their thoughts. Consequently, malicious thoughts, desires, and acts do not arouse a poisonous condition and disturb normal bodily functions. Thus, they are born, they live, and they die, according to their nature.

This illustration prepares for a statement and a consideration of the Law. Man is body, mind, and spirit; and within the three is that which we call the Divine Spark, or the soul. This divine spark, being of God and making man different from the animal, is that something which receives and stores impressions. It is the Reflector. All that the divine entity receives it will reflect. This reflection is shown in the body of man, for the body is the temple of God, the temple of the soul. But in those beings in whom there is no divine spark, in whom there is no reflector, as is also the case with animals, even though the nature is vicious, viciousness is not reflected in the personality and in the body, except possibly to make it more nearly perfect; for the natural animal is always perfect in its physical being.

The doctrine may seem hard; but it is in perfect harmony with the teachings of God, with the teachings of philosophers and Masters, and absolutely in harmony with the teachings of Nature. Nature recognizes no soul in her creation; nevertheless, her manifestations are perfect. Man alone, having free-will and the spark of the divine, shows what kind of a creator he is, and reflects in his body the character of his acts, his desires, and his thoughts. The animal, on the other hand, being the product of nature alone, always manifests perfection because she is perfect, though changeable and never individualized in entities that continue permanently.

## CHAPTER FIFTEEN

## THERE IS NO REASON FOR MAN TO BE SICK

Why should man be sick? Why should he be living in sin?

There is no logical reason why man should not be living the higher life. That is, there is no reason why man should live a life that is sinful, nor is there any logical reason why he should be sick.

Sin and sickness are really one and the same thing. The one results in the other. The fact is, sin- which is nothing more nor less than wrong living and wrong doing- is the cause of sickness, and, in the end, brings death as the final penalty.

Sin is classed as sin because it is the opposite of good. It is sin not because God has said that man should not do thus and so, not because theology outlines it as sin, nor because philosophers have said that to do certain things is to commit sin; but it is sin because it brings pain or sorrow, loss or misery, harm or injury, either to the one that commits it or to the one against whom it is committed. There is no other basis for sin than this. Therefore, sin is simply wrong doing or wrong living. Why should man do the things that are wrong. Simply because he has a mistaken idea in regard to life and conduct, an idea that has become a race belief and therefore a part of his nature. He has the mistaken notion that to do certain things will be to his advantage, will bring him profit or pleasure or honor. He does these things not because he wants to do them but because he has been gradually led to believe that only in this way can he obtain the things that he desires.

There are actually few men who do wrong because of a love for the wrong. It is to be admitted, however, that there are men who do wrong because they love the wrong. Human nature is capable of being perverted. There are those whom we call degenerate because they actually love to do that which natural and divine law points out as being wrong. They delight in doing things which are contrary to the laws of nature and the laws of God. They take pleasure in doing that which nature revolts at doing. But the class of society known as degenerates is in the minority and cannot be taken as a standard. The vast majority of mankind love the right. They do wrong only through the mistaken idea that what they are doing will bring honor, ease, success, or other desirable things.

Doing those things which in the mind and the heart are known to be wrong and out of harmony with the Law, doing them even with superficial thought and indifferent purpose- this it is which leaves its mark upon the body of man, and results in sickness and death.

Who is there that does not know that anger is wrong, that it actually does no good, that it can not make a wrong right? Humanity in general knows this. It is generally recognized that anger in itself is poisonous to mind and body, that it is a destructive power. Yet how many are there who control their anger? It is this which constitutes sin; to know that it is wrong, wrong not simply by reason of becoming angry, but wrong because anger in itself is a poison and a destructive power; to know that anger is wrong and yet to give it place in one's life- this constitutes sin. By becoming angry, man liberates in his organism and sets into motion poisonous vibrations. This results in a disturbed condition of the organism and even induces illness. By virtue of this fact is anger sin. The results and the effects of an act or of a state of mind determine whether it is to be classed as sin or righteousness, as wrong or right. Thus it is a truth that sin is sickness or that sickness is sin. Had the person not become angry and thus poisoned the life blood, the particular ailment that resulted from the poisonous state would not have come upon him.

Again, who does not know that jealousy results in no good, that it can not remove the object of jealousy? Who does not understand that jealousy generates a poison which causes a diseased condition of the organism? Not the mere fact of being jealous constitutes sin. The fact that jealousy is a destructive power, that it does harm- this makes jealousy a sin. The fact that the harm coming to the system through jealousy affects the soul- this makes jealousy a sin. Again, sin and sickness are seen to be the same thing, each, a reflection of the other.

Thus it is with all the great passions, such as, hate, jealousy, malice, ill-will, and other dark and deadly feelings. They are destructive and poisonous in their character, and are therefore classed as sinful. But it is the same with the minor passions, those which spring from the greater. It is possible for the minor passions to be so covered up that they are hardly recognized. Nevertheless, they are deadly in their ultimate results.

But what is the remedy for these sins, these destructive forces?

The answer is simple and plain, and comes thundering down the cycles of time: Love, Forgiveness, and Good-will.

Love, Forgiveness, and Good-will are the divine passions, the cardinal virtues. It is these which will ultimately destroy all gross and destructive passions. As man becomes truly developed, he will change gross and destructive passions into divine passions. into creative and developing power, and into constructive forces.

But, says the seeker, Why should I love those who try to destroy my happiness, those who sin against me, those who aim at ruining; those who would defame me?

But why should you hate them that hate you? Do you think that hating them in return will change them? Will it cause them to stop hating you? Do you imagine that your hatred will do them any harm or that it will do you any good? Not at all. Except in very rare cases will your hatred do them harm or serve as a punishment to them. It will only stimulate and intensify and exaggerate their hatred of you, thus making matters worse. It will by no means diminish their hatred of you. Nor will it do yourself any possible good. But it will do positive harm to yourself; for it will poison mind, and soul, and body.

On the other hand, if you v/ere to change your hatred into love, the beneficent results to yourself would be intensified and doubled. In the first place, your own love and good-will toward them will act as an attracting power, which draws out whatever good is in them, slowly it may be at first, but surely; and in time it will bring you their good-will, at least it will cause them to reflect, and to give up their evil designs against you. In the second place, your own hate changed into love acts as a vivifying power to yourself; and, instead of bringing illness and depression and sorrow, it brings more of health, more of love, and more of life. Whereas hatred and ill-will arouse poisonous conditions resulting in disease and distress, forgiveness and good-will is a health-inspiring tonic that promotes poise, peace, and health of body and mind. It may require a mighty mental effort to give love and forgiveness in exchange for grudges, hatred, and ill-will. But the reward is proportionate to the effort, the gain is worth the price.

As it is with the passion hatred, so is it with all other passions of destructive, negative nature. By being changed into life-giving, constructive passions, they bring good in return for that which would otherwise be destructive. As soon as men come to understand this truth they will honor the Law of Transmutation, which enables them to transmute the dross of error and sin into the pure gold of love and forgiveness and good-will. As soon as men realize that destructive passions do no good, that by indulging in them one can not change the plans or the feelings of others, then will they put forth effort to become free from the power of every type of evil passion. Gradually they will be enabled to give up sin; and, with sin out of the way, sickness can not long remain.

Now; in respect to sickness and the statement that sin is the cause of sickness, whether the sin be on our part or that of another, it is to be freely admitted that sin may be committed innocently or ignorantly. Nevertheless, every wrong, every act that is out of harmony with natural or divine law. is a sin and reaps the reward or the result according to his nature. It is a recognized fact that ignorance of the Law excuses no one. For this reason, it behooves each one to understand the Law. The sooner we understand the requirements of the Law, the sooner shall we be free from all those things which are undesirable. Chief among the conditions from which knowledge of the Law and obedience to it will set us free are sickness, sorrow, and failure.

The object of life should be to become free from ignorance and error; to understand the Law; to become accurate in discrimination for the sake of choosing the things that are constructive and upbuilding and life-giving, for the sake of rejecting the things that are destructive to life and all that is dear to life. Having learned these things, it is for us to live according to the constructive principle so that we may be continually improving the temple of life, and increasing the resisting, life-giving forces within us. This pertains not only to the body but to the soul as well. Life of the body alone is animal life. Life of body and soul is divine life; and no one can be truly human or truly god-like unless he honors life of body and soul alike, regarding one equal to the other in importance.

This is what Jesus called "the holy life." Living thus, honoring divine and natural law in daily life, attaining Illumination of Soul- this the Master Jesus called "receiving the Holy Ghost." For when men cleanse the body, and free the soul from its grave of earth; when they free the body from sin and from sickness- then do they reach Illumination, then do they receive the greater life, then do they enter here and now into the kingdom of heaven.

The Illuminati teach that the holy life is in the beginning a life of faith. Unless the one who desires the benefits of the holy life is willing so to live as to receive the benefits, in full and complete faith that he shall receive, there can be no results. But the Illuminati emphasize more especially that, when man awakens to these great truths, when he sees that it is to his benefit to live in harmony with the Law, it is necessary for him to have faith sufficiently strong to enable him to continue living the life. Eventually, having made the beginning, he will become established in faith and in life, and the results of his faith and of his living will become unmistakably manifest.

Then he will no longer need to live by faith alone. For he lives through knowledge of the power. It is knowledge undeniable because he realizes results from living the life. Gradually, the holy life becomes his natural, normal mode of living, and ultimately brings him into consciousness of the Godhead, and into conscious oneness with the Divine Creator, Ruler of all things.

Thus also is it with the sick and the afflicted. In the beginning, it is faith, faith with some degree of effort, it may be. The sufferer must have faith in God and in His promises. He must begin to educate and to train his thoughts, his desires, and his conduct in harmony with the Law, natural and divine. Gradually, the new life will set him free from disease and suffering, and will lead him to Illumination, to the holy life, the life without sin, Life Immortal and Eternal.

We are not to think of God as the One who has power to free us from sickness and from sin. Rather, He is the One who has made man in His own image, and has endowed him with power to free himself from sin, power to cut the bonds that bind him to ignorance and error and sin, power to sever the chains that hold him to the earth and to all that is earthly. God is all power- this we must admit. But God does not use His power to help us. He delegates to us the right and the privilege of using His power so that we may become free and manifest the Godhood within.

It is as if our earthly parent, having abundant possessions, should give us the right to draw upon his resources. We have perfect right to draw upon his account to the full extent of our need. But, according to the conditions specified by our parent, he will not bring us the money, or give it to us, or help us to get it, even though we may be in great need or in distress. His provision is this: "My son, there is plenty for you and for me. The fund is here. It is for you to draw upon as freely and as liberally as you desire. You are at perfect liberty to draw therefrom whatever you need. If you have not faith in my word, if you have not energy to accept the freedom I offer, then I can not help you."

The power of God is sufficient to free all mankind from disease and from sorrow, from misery and from death. But He does not force His healing power. His saving grace, upon any man. He does, however, give man the privilege of drawing therefrom all that he needs. This stipulation, nevertheless, is attached: man must meet certain conditions in regard to thought and conduct; also, he must have faith sufficient to enable him to begin drawing on the account of the Infinite. As faith increases, the greater will be his power to lay hold of the resources of Infinite Goodness. These truths the Illuminati teach. The teacher-healer makes it a special point to teach the true doctrine of life to those who are sick and suffering, to those who are in sin and in sorrow. Not only does he teach, but he gives help whenever possible. Those who are ready to receive shall be given the sublime instructions. The teacher-healer points the way, the way not only to freedom for body but to freedom for the soul. Mankind shall be taught what to believe and how to live the Holy Life, the Life that gives freedom and Illumination, the Life that leads to Soul Consciousness and to Sonship with the Father. Soul Science is the Way to Life and Immortality.

## CHAPTER SIXTEEN

## GOD AND NATURE, THE ONLY PHYSICIANS

Man is of two constituent parts, each as important as the other. His body, the material nature, corresponds to the earth, and is under the control of nature. His soul, the spiritual being, corresponds to God, and is under his guidance.

In saying that the body is ruled over by nature, and the soul by God, it must be understood that reference is made to the true man, the man not controlled or guided or ruled over by carnal desires.

Contrary to many metaphysical schools, the Illuminati maintain that the flesh is as real and as important as the soul or the spirit of man. In fact, they maintain that the material is but another expression of spirit, a lower grade of the universal substance, that it is even necessary as a medium through which the soul may express itself. Furthermore, they maintain that nature is not the enemy of man, but that she is his guide, "the great physician" to the flesh of man, just as God is guide and physician to his soul. Body and soul are equally important. Each is essential to the other. The two should be in equilibrium, then is man a perfect being.

That which is called disease may be of body or of mind or it may be of both mind and body. It may be purely of the flesh or it may be purely of the soul. Again, it may be, and often is, of both. The true physician, the true healer, will give careful consideration to both soul and body; for he understands that man is ruled either by one or by the other, or, in some cases, by the two in combination, and that his remedies must affect both.

It is not always true that Nature, even if given an opportunity, will heal the sick; for Nature alone does not reach the soul of man, though she w^ill do her best to heal the body. If the soul of man is ill from erroneous and perverted beliefs, thoughts, and desires, Nature alone can net effect a cure. The healing of an afflicted soul is affected by God through the instrumentality of man who has a wise philosophy, a Wisdom Religion, to give to troubled souls.

There can be no question that man will accept Soul Science as a religion when its principles are fully understood; for it is a rational and natural, though withal a mystic, religion.

Fundamental among the principles of Soul Science, as advocated by the Illuminati, is the doctrine that the material, the physical, the flesh, is real, as real as are the spirit and the soul of man. The spirit and the soul of man can, to a great extent, minister to the material, to the body; but, in the main, Nature is the physician to the body of man. Nature, as a healer, includes all that concerns physical needs, as, food, clothing, exercise, work, rest, relaxation, recreation, bathing, breathing, and other normal and natural conditions of life. Although the body is real and by no means is to be underestimated in its importance, yet the true man, the divine element, is the soul. The soul is that which manifests through the flesh. The body is the vehicle of expression for the soul. Flesh, under physical environments, is the only avenue through which Soul can attain its divine heritage of Conscious Unity with God.

There are many diseases of the mind which can be cured only through the forces of the heart and the soul. There are many diseases of the body caused by a diseased mind and soul. These, with the help of Nature, can be cured only through the efforts of the Soul that has become enlightened. Soul Science denies absolutely that the material part of man's being is unreal and that it has no existence. It teaches conclusively that the material is as truly real in existence as the spirit and the soul, and that it is as truly necessary as are the spirit and the soul. It further holds that only through the material form is it possible for the spirit and the soul of man to manifest. Aye, even more, only through the material form of man is it possible for God Himself to manifest. Therefore, man honors God not by denouncing the body, but by exalting it; not by denying existence of the body, but by raising it to a state of perfection. In order to glorify God, man must honor body as well as soul. He must make them co-equal in development. In other words, the highest development is reached when man establishes an equilibrium between body and soul, the spirit of God being the central or pivotal point.

The general principles of Soul Science have received attention elsewhere. In consideration of the topic, "God and Nature, the only physicians," it is fitting to employ a lull and detailed illustration of the treatment that an Illuminati, or a Soul Science, Healer would give a sufferer. Take, for example, the treatment of a typical case of the white Plague- Consumption- greatest of all scourges.

First, consider the cause of this disease. In the main, the Illuminati agree with scientists who have given careful investigation to the cause of this dread affliction. Consumption is a disease that forms waste, or pus matter, at the expense of healthy tissues, even feeding upon healthy tissues to form pus. The formation of pus is accomplished through a state of congestion. Herein is found both the cause and the basis of cure.

Congestion results from a stoppage in the normal processes of elimination. The principle of a congested state finds natural illustration in a sewerage system. So long as the sewer is kept open the waste flows freely. But, if no attention is given to the passage, and if there is a surplus of waste material, a clogged condition, or congestion, results. Experience shows that the effects of a congested state are in all cases the same. The congestion becomes heated through a state of fermentation. This produces morbid matter, which becomes a poison. That which takes place in the sewer takes place in man's organism, and the results are the same.

Universally, man eats too much- that is, he takes in a greater amount of food than is required by the system. Thus, his system becomes overloaded and all the functions of his organism are overtaxed in their effort to throw off the ill effects of this surplus. This fact- the fact that almost universally man loads his system with an unnecessary amount of food- is admitted by practically all scientists and physicians.

Another fact should be noted, that man does not keep his system in condition to throw off the surplus material. The result is the same as in the case of a congested sewer. The unnecessary material is retained in the system. It produces an unnatural heat. In some part of the body congestion results. Heat intensifies, and the morbid material is turned into pus. This affects the surrounding tissues, and disease follows.

Various diseases result from this condition. The cause is the same; but, being in different parts of the body, the disease receives different names. According to statistics, the most common trouble is consumption. The reason fur this is seen in the fact that the waste material most naturally settles in the lungs. Why? Simply because the blood carrying food material passes through the lungs, where, according to Nature's purpose, it is supposed to be charged with new life, and health-inspiring properties. But, unlike all other animals, man, as a rule, does not breathe properly. Being an artificial breather, and not taking in a sufficient amount of vivifying and purifying air, he is not able to throw off the poison resulting from all accumulation of waste material. Consequently, it settles in the lungs and bronchial tubes, and the result is tuberculosis.

Having given brief consideration to the cause, it remains to consider the cure of this dread disease. In the first place, this is a disease of the body; but it has been brought on either through ignorance of nature's laws or through deliberate violation of them. Being a physical derangement primarily, it is only natural to draw the inference that Nature alone can effect a cure, and that the mind and the soul are of little consequence in treating this difficulty.

Such an inference, however, is erroneous in the extreme, for the reason that consumption is distinctively a negative disease, and is accompanied by a negative, inert state of mind. Notwithstanding the fact that the average consumptive believes he will eventually be restored to health and strength, he is disinclined to put forth the least effort to regain health and strength. The average consumptive is particularly affected by a disinclination, an unwillingness, or even an aversion, to doing the things that are conducive to improvement of health. Activity and exercise, so much needed in order to stimulate expansive power in the lungs, are distasteful. In some cases, air, light, and sunshine- Nature's prime restoring agencies- seem to irritate and annoy. Lethargy, indifference and sluggishness are prominent traits, and stomp the disease as particularly negative in its symptoms. Consequently, in the treatment of this disease, Nature must be supplemented by both mind and soul.

It is important to arouse and to stimulate the patient's mind, heart, and soul. He must be convinced that mind, heart, and soul are indispensable factors in healing. He must realize that man is created in the image of God, the Father, and that he honors and glorifies his Maker by perfecting the divine image in which he is created. He must realize that, by allowing the image of God to become disease-racked, he is dishonoring the Creator, and that, in so doing, he is committing a sin as truth, as if he were deliberately violating a moral or a legal code. The patient's moral and spiritual sense of responsibility must be aroused. He must see and understand that illness is actual sin, or the result of actual sin. To disobey a law of health is as grievous as any other form of unrighteousness. As he is responsible for having disregarded the laws of health, so now it is his duty to restore conditions of health, and to live in harmony with nature's laws.

It is well for the patient to know that violation of nature's laws in regard to health is a form of unrighteousness. But it may be wise to impress on his mind the positive statements of the principle, and to emphasize the desirability of righteousness rather than the undesirability of error, sin, and unrighteousness. Let him see that faithful observance of the laws of health is as truly a form of righteousness as is observance of the moral Decalogue. Especially if the sufferer is religiously inclined he should be led to see that righteousness includes observance of hygienic laws, including such homely items as correct habits in regard to diet, sleep, exercise, work, recreation, bathing, and breathing.

In arousing the sufferer's mind to a realization of responsibility, emphasis should be placed on the thought of privilege, and on the desirability and the possibility of health, strength, and vigor. Caution should be taken to prevent him from settling into morbid reflection on the error of his ways. Cause of illness should instantly take the turn of rectifying illness. The only reason for a patient's knowing the cause of illness is to enable him to remove the cause. He must understand that reversing conditions and removing causes are the only rational means of restoring health and strength. Ambition must be quickened. Faith in the possibility of health and strength must be intensified. Interest in a worthy work or cause; the consciousness of being valuable to family, neighbors, and friends; the desire to accomplish a cherished purpose; activities which absorb his attention and interest, and which take his thought away from petty symptoms-these are items which enable mind and soul to cooperate with nature's healing agencies.

The principles and the arguments of Soul Science can be used to good advantage in stimulating mind and soul of the patient to normal activity. He should be convinced that it is not the divine purpose for man to suffer and die, but that it is according to the plan of the Infinite for him to live a useful life and thus to glorify his Maker. A reasonable amount of the Illuminati series of literature may be placed in his hands.

At the same time that the mind and the soul are being fed and aroused to activity the physician or healer must give careful attention to the physical being of the sufferer.

First in importance is it to free his organism of the congestion, the decayed food material that is stored up in his system. This is accomplished by two methods, which should be followed at the same time. The first method is through the medium of daily warm baths, both external and internal; the second is through cutting down the allowance of food, not eating so often nor so much, and giving special attention to the quality of food and the proper combination of foods.

Under this treatment, two full meals a day or three light meals are sufficient. The morning meal should be light, but of the most nourishing material. Take barley that is not pearled to the amount of a cup full, pour over it two cups of cold water. Let it stand over night. In the morning, this should be stirred up thoroughly so as to release from the barley the natural salts. Then pour the water off, to this add the whites of two eggs thoroughly beaten, and add a little cream. This is sufficient for breakfast. Nothing more should be eaten until noon in order that the patient may become thoroughly hungry.

The noon meal should consist of a good combination of three classes of foods: first, a foundation, or a vitalizing and nourishing food, as, barley, beans, peas, wheat, lentils; second, a cleansing cooked vegetable, as, turnips, parsnips, spinach, tomatoes; third, a stimulating, appetizing, uncooked vegetable, as, lettuce, celery, olives. Whole wheat bread is to be used in addition to other foods. Barley for the noon meal should be soaked before being cooked. It should be well boiled. A dressing for it can be made of cream, with the white of eggs, and some good fat, such as, olive oil, butter, or peanut oil. This may be made according to the taste of the patient. Vegetables and grains should be thoroughly cooked, in fact, so thoroughly that they form a sort of puree.

This general outline of combinations admits of good variety so that the one following the treatment need not tire of any article of food. Frequently changes may be made. Yet the three classes of foods should be represented at each meal. The nourishing or vitalizing product should be chosen as a foundation for the meal, then a cooked vegetable of cleansing and eliminating value according to taste. Lettuce, celery, or olives, as an appetizing and stimulating food, have qualities that are highly beneficial. Of the vegetables, spinach should be used most frequently because it contains vegetable salts required by the system.

White bread should not be used, nor should white potatoes form a part of the menu. These are forbidden because they clog the system with unnecessary starchy material. They are like vampires to the organic lime in the organism, of which the starved and depleted system of the consumptive is in particular need.

A word in regard to meat. The Illuminati do not endorse a meat diet. Nevertheless, they are not so radical and so unreasonable as to expect men, especially the afflicted, to give up meat all at once. Nor do they consider it wisdom for a person to make a sudden, abrupt change in a habit of long standing. It is to be noted that nature's changes are slow and gradual. Man should learn from nature and from his Creator. Seeing that nature's ways are processes of time, it is well for man to follow the example of nature in this respect. Taking men as they are, and seeing that the vast majority are meat eaters, the Illuminati advocate gradual changes toward the non-meat diet. In the process of change from one system of living to another, especially in the case of a patient, the Illuminati forbid the meats that are the most harmful and allow the use of the least harmful. Therefore, they recommend that the patient use only mutton and fowl, and that the barley, beans, or peas be cooked with the meat. In this way, the meat need not be eaten, as, through the process of cooking, the essence is extracted from the meat, and is in the soup and absorbed by the vegetable. That which remains of the meat, if eaten, would only tax the system, would be of no benefit, and would increase congestion.

In the evening, the patient should be allowed only barley water and the whites of eggs, with some whole wheat bread, only in an amount sufficient to satisfy, but not enough to congest the system. Never, under any circumstances, should the patient retire soon after a full meal. The evening meal should be so arranged that the food is thoroughly digested before it is time to retire. Then, just before retiring, the juice of grape fruit, apple, or pineapple may be taken. The fruit should be thoroughly masticated, and the pulp rejected, only the juice being swallowed.

In order to effect a cure, it is important for the patient to be exceedingly hungry at meal time; but he should eat only enough to satisfy. Between meals fruits should be taken, such as apples, pine apples, grape fruit, and other desirable fruits. Water may be used freely and at any time except with meals. Fruit juices, however, are better than water for the reason that they contain the salts that are required by the debilitated system.

The one who is physically impaired, whether from consumption, cancer, nerve exhaustion, or any other chronic ailment, will find it an excellent plan to eat stewed apples before retiring. These contain every salt required by the system. The apples should be carefully selected and prepared. They should not be peeled, nor should the core be removed; for in the skin there is a valuable salt, and in the core there is an active bitter principle which is of great value. The apple should be quartered so as to allow examination of it, and any undesirable part may be removed. They should be cooked, without sugar, until they are very soft, forming a thick pulp or jelly. When cool they are ready to serve. This is not only a tasty but a most valuable food. It is not supposed that the core or the skin are to be swallowed, but simply chewed so as to extract the food value, only the juice and pure pulp being swallowed. Contrary to popular opinion, apples served in this manner are not bitter and disagreeable, but are really delicious when properly prepared. It is well for all, whether physically impaired or not, to make frequent use of apples prepared in this manner.

It is a mistake to serve apples with sugar and cream. Sugar robs them of the natural lime, while the cream makes a combination that can be digested only by the strongest stomach.

Regulation of diet is only one means by which nature effects a cure, and it is imperative that the: patient shall be active and zealous in promoting such conditions as shall enable nature to perfect her work of healing. If the patient is careless and indifferent in regard to hygienic requirements, if he follows the healer's advice with irregularity, indulging his own whims at will, he can expect nothing but irregularity and unsatisfactory progress. For this reason a disease of negative type demands firm cooperation of the patient with natural means of healing. Heart, mind, soul, and body must be co-partners with God and Nature. It is easy to say that God and Nature are the only true healers. As an unqualified statement, it may seem to be an easy philosophy that declares God and Nature to be the only healers. Yet faith, courage, firmness, patience, and perseverance are required on man's part to enable him to make such conditions that God and Nature can perfect their work. Patient as well as physician must work in harmony with God and Nature. The Illuminati physician is supposed to have given time and attention to the study of Nature's laws and ways. He has formulated natural methods of treatment. The patient is responsible for faithfulness in observing the requirements of a natural system of treatment.

# THE WAY TO LIFE AND IMMORTALITY

Equally important with the question of diet is that of breathing. The patient must be led to see the importance of full, deep breathing. It is well for him to fol- low exercises which require him to breathe in harmony with Sacred Mantrams. This practice insures rhythmical as well as deep breathing. Particularly one whose lungs are affected should cultivate habits of correct breathing in order to throw out the poison from his system. Otherwise, the state of congestion continues. Habits in regard to sleeping are also of importance. The patient should have eight hours of sleep in a room in which there is plenty of fresh air. The windows should be open night as well as day, in winter as well as in summer.

A natural system of treatment of disease gives attention to exercise, as an essential to health and vigor.

Outdoor exercise is best. Walking is advisable. Horse-back riding is particularly good. Often it is only by sheer force that the patient can be induced to take any kind of wholesome exercise. For this reason a philosophy that arouses and stimulates a fondness for activity is of incalculable benefit. The real self, the true being, the Immortal part of his nature, should be quickened to consciousness and to activity. This will stimulate an inclination to put forth effort, it will arouse fondness for wholesome exertion. It will make industry and employment attractive, and counteract the tendency to lethargy and sluggishness which is a noticeable trait of those who suffer from an affliction of the lungs.

If the patient is faithful to natural methods of treatment as regards food, drink, sleep, work, exercise, rest, recreation; if he makes constant friends of light, air, and sunshine; if he cultivates wholesome habits of thought, and eliminates from his mind every type of bitterness and envy- there is no reason why God and Nature should not effect in him a perfect cure. It is not too much to claim that every case of consumption, if treated according to these principles, may be cured unless the disease has so ravaged the system that there is no chance for freeing it from the congestion. This claim may seem extreme. Nevertheless, it is not greater than the truth. It seems extreme only because the treatment has not been generally accepted.

Another disease that is causing great ravages among mankind is cancer. Like consumption, cancer is a negative condition. Both the cause and the method of cure are, in general, similar to those outlined for consumption. The congested condition that causes cancer settles in other parts of the body and the manner of destruction is different; consequently, it receives a different name.)

Treatment of disease according to natural means may seem crude to the radical seeker after mysticism who believes the mind is all-sufficient, and that faith alone is necessary for the cure of disease. But the rational, well-balanced mind will recognize that natural means combined with a reasonable faith in God and Nature is the true method. It gives due credit to power of mind and soul. It recognizes both God and Nature, both divine and human agencies, both spirit and matter. It is based on the philosophy that God and Nature are the true healers. But it points out the way by which man may cooperate with God and Nature, and thus make it possible for them to perfect their office as healers of men.

## CHAPTER SEVENTEEN

## TO THE BODY, NATURE IS THE PHYSICIAN

In this connection, Nature includes air, food, drink, exercise and recreation, baths for cleanliness and rejuvenation of the body, sunshine, and all those things which sustain the life of the body, and which give health, strength, and vitality to the physical man.

Strange as it may seem, there are some called mystics and metaphysicians who, though denying that the physical or material man has real existence, admit that food, drink, and air are necessary to the body. Yet these same metaphysicians fail to recognize that the quality of food and drink has anything to do with the welfare of the body. That it is possible for such a belief to have place in the minds of men, even the highly educated, is to be explained in the fact that the race mind has accepted an inconsistent religion or none at all. The average mind has not been willing to think, to investigate, or to analyze for itself.

But the time is now here when man will no longer bow down to a philosophy or a religion merely because a teacher of prominence promulgates it. He demands a religion or a philosophy that will stand the test of reason and analysis, one that recognizes Nature as well as God, one that considers Nature and God as co-workers, co-creators, life-givers on an equality with each other. The Illuminati maintain that Nature is the spouse, the hand- maid of God, equally important with Him, because all laws work in unity, yet only through duality. On the human plane, body and soul hold a similar relationship with each other, each being equally necessary, equally important to man. In regard to the body, Nature must be consulted and obeyed. God is the physician to the soul, often to the body as well. Nature's laws, however, in the healing of mind and soul, must be honored and obeyed. Nature and God work in unison.

In their Soul Science instructions, the Illuminati recognize that there is in reality only one disease; but, like all things else in nature, this disease manifests itself in various ways. This one ill, this one affliction, may be either of the mind or of the body. It may be caused either by wrong thoughts and desires or by a wrong mode of living, through ignorance of nature's laws or through willful violation of them. Or, as indeed is true in most cases, it may be due to a complication of physical and mental errors.

The millions are living in ignorance of the principles that underlie proper foods and proper combinations of foods. Many are better informed in regard to the treatment of animals and proper nourishment for them than they are in regard to the care of their own families. Many make a careful study of the conditions that develop live stock to the highest point of beauty and perfection; wherehas, in regard to their families, they are content to live according to the custom of their ancestors, regardless of the wisdom or the advisability of such custom.

The blood coursing through the veins of man is his life; but blood can be healthful and vitalizing and pure only as it is made from proper foods. It is impossible to have pure blood unless proper nourishment is taken. Noble character of thoughts and desires, no matter how pure and holy and lofty they may be, alone, can not insure good pure blood. This the Illuminati teach as a fundamental law- that mental and physical conditions must supplement each other; that mind alone is not all-powerful; that thought alone can not effect perfect physical states. Therefore, they contend that food, pure in quality and harmonious in combination, is essential to good health.

More than this, in their teaching in regard to correct habits of living, they advocate that there is a proper and an improper time for eating. In general, the time for eating is indicated by nature's call- the state of hunger. To eat when one is not hungry is doing nothing less than storing disease in one's system. Nature has so constituted man and his organs that there will be no digestive fluids in the stomach and the intestines unless he is actually hungry. Consequently, without hunger, the system is not in condition to make digestion and assimilation possible.

If food is taken into the stomach when it is not ready to receive food, digestion is delayed. There being heat in the stomach, the food becomes heated and may even become putrid. The result is that the digested food and the fluids to be assimilated, instead of being healthy and full of life-giving power, become a poison. Only the resisting power of the body prevents man from quickly succumbing to these toxic poisons. It may be years before the body falls in death through their effects; or there may be years of suffering from various diseases. It is now fully recognized that many cases of insanity are due to auto-intoxication. Auto-intoxication is simply a poisoning of the system through indiscreet habits of eating. It may be due to an excess of food, or to an improper combination of food, or to an inferior quality of food, or to food not adapted to the person's particular need. Under these conditions, the material is not digested or assimilated, neither is it passed out of the system. This results in the manufacture of toxins which are retained in the organism, keeping it in a poisoned state.

Correct habits in regard to diet, however, is only one of nature's means of maintaining health and strength. An other is in regard to breathing. No one can be healthy and strong who does not breathe freely and deeply of pure fresh air. It is true that men have lived many years who did not breathe properly; and even those who live indoors almost entirely attain a ripe old age. But it is not possible to determine how much longer they might have lived had they been subject to normal conditions. If man were to breathe deeply and properly, and have fresh air at all times, it would be possible for him to make use of inferior foods, even foods that are now a poison to him.

# THE WAY TO LIFE AND IMMORTALITY

When the food essences pass through the lungs, the deep breathing of pure air would extract the poison from them and throw it out of the system. Nevertheless, even though this is possible, yet it is by no means advisable to tax the lungs with unnecessary work in this way. It is, however, a fact worth knowing; for most of us are at times so situated that we can not avail ourselves of proper foods. Under temporary conditions of this kind, we need have no fear of harmful results if we consciously cooperate with the lungs in freeing the system of deleterious substances. But, since man is ordinarily an artificial breather, elimination of poisons is not accomplished by the lungs. Poisonous substances therefore must be eliminated in some other way, as, through the skin, the kidneys, or the bowels. Otherwise, they remain in the system, disturbing the whole being.

As pure food and pure air are essential to all men in the flesh, whether they are the highest mystics or the humblest artisans, so is sunshine also necessary. For it is through the rays of the sun that man receives vitality, a magnetism that makes for life and power just as the sun's rays shining on the earth enable it to produce abundantly the plants and the herbs required by all living creatures. Were it not for the rays of the sun striking the earth and having connection with it and charging it with life-power, all vegetation would be poisonous. It is a note-worthy fact that deadly weeds grow under trees and in dense forests where the rays of the sun do not penetrate. That sunshine is essential to physical welfare is recognized by practically every Sanitarium. Sun parlors afford the patient opportunity for basking in the sun's rays and becoming charged with new life and vigor.

Sleep is another of nature's means of promoting health and vigor. For centuries, it has been taken for granted that the strength of man is derived from the food that he eats; but this is no longer regarded as an' exact statement of truth. Men have overlooked the importance of sleep in its bearing on strength and vitality. Food, like fire in the engine, produces heat and motive power; but the power is secured from the water in the engine which becomes heated and generates steam. Thus, the food that is eaten, by creating the proper heat, is simply the means of furnishing the power. During sleep, when assimilation takes place, and when fresh pure air is breathed in, the body receives the strength and the power that gives life and vigor. Thus, sleep is an essential to health, strength, and vitality.

Nevertheless, perfect relaxation and wholesome sleep are dependent upon other conditions, particularly upon dietary discretion and upon an abundance of pure fresh air. There can be no health-inspiring sleep if digestion is not normal. When there is an assimilation of toxins instead of life-giving material, sleep is not perfect. If there is lack of pure fresh air in the sleeping chamber natural combustion is interfered with. When there are no drafts in the stove the fires die out. There should be an abundant circulation of pure fresh air in the human organism to insure the fires that aid in assimilation and in the storing up of vitality.

Dietary indiscretion is not the only cause of illness, nor is restoration to normal dietary conditions the only means of regaining health and efficiency. Dietary discretion, an abundant supply of pure fresh air, wholesome sleep, frequent access to the genial rays of the sun, normal exercise and activity- all are essentials to physical and mental health and efficiency. Yet, neither one alone is sufficient. A rational, harmonious combination of all these items, however, will work wonders in establishing health and strength. Then, combine with these measures, the power of wholesome, constructive, optimistic thought-habits and the power of a masterful will, and you have a rational system of living. All these conditions should be observed by the natural man. Nor is it at all difficult to do so, though it may seem difficult to those who have lived unnaturally, lo, these many years.

It is no more difficult to have the proper food for breakfast than to have unnatural foods. Nor is it more difficult to prepare them. Nor indeed is it more expensive. However, if man observes the natural laws he will eat but little in the morning. His morning meal will consist of the juices of fruits, or the waters of barley or wheat, or other liquid foods in which are found the natural salts-givers of life.

It is not nature's plan that man should partake of heavy food before working. This is indicated by the fact that man is not actually hungry on first arising in the morning. It is admitted that he may have a desire for food, that he may have an appetite, early in the morning. But desires and appetite are not from nature but from custom. No one in a normal condition has actual hunger on first arising in the morning. In this fact is the proof that it is not natural for one to eat at that time. Yet it is found that, unless one is entirely morbid or in a state of ill-health, one does have a natural thirst soon after arising. This is an indication that one needs some liquid- either pure water or fruit juices or waters that contain the life-giving salts of grains. By partaking of a simple, wholesome drink of this nature, man prepares his system for the noon meal. Toward noon, being hungry, which indicates that the digestive juices are active, he is in good condition for a full meal, well-balanced and harmonious in combination. Thus, there is no reason why digestion should not be normal, and assimilation perfect, resulting in pure blood and a state of perfect health.

Taken as a class, however, men are in a state of poor health even though they may not be aware of the fact. Often they are not hungry at noon, and make the mistake of eating at the call of desire and appetite rather than of hunger. To eat when not hungry may satisfy an abnormal craving, but it also adds poison to the system and only gives more fuel for disease to do its destructive work. It is hardly possible to lay too much stress on the importance of dietary discretion. Practically, the whole of life depends on the food one eats. More ills of life are due to improper food than mankind dreams of. An excess of stimulating food creates a desire for alcoholic drinks; or, it may arouse to an abnormal degree the carnal nature, and intensify tendencies toward crime and lust. In either case, the evil is entirely dependent for its existence on the heat that is generated in the body by improper foods. Heat thus generated is not normal. It leads to an unnatural craving. It may be a craving for strong drink. It may be an abnormal passion in the generative system, which creates an uncontrollable desire for lustful acts. Thus, the twin evils- drunkenness and tariff in white slaves- are traceable chiefly to dietary indiscretion. One will exist as long as the other. And neither the one nor the other will be overcome or can possibly be thoroughly overcome until man eats according to rational, scientific dietary principles.

When man and woman eat according to reason and good judgment, and when they observe other natural laws, the heat generated in the system and communicated to the brain will be normal. The demands of the body, however, will not be destroyed or weakened or impaired. Rather, as a result of discretion in regard to food, they will be natural and trustworthy and will require only normal reasonable satisfaction.

The Illuminati do not deal with results. They aim, instead, to correct the root of troubles. Social evils, like cancer, may be apparently removed while in reality the root of the difficulty remains in the organism. So long as there is one root remaining in the social body, it is liable to grow again; and, like cancer, every new growth will be more virulent than former ones.

For this reason, the Illuminati maintain that neither the evils of alcohol nor the evils of prostitution can be removed through legislative acts. Nor can desires be controlled by legal enactments or by legislative power in the hands of associated physicians, no matter how extensive may be their learning. Such evils, all evils, can be removed only by giving knowledge to mankind and by removing the cause. The cause of evils is twofold- primary and secondary. The cause reveals itself in the way man lives, in his manner of eating, sleeping, breathing, exercising, working. Such things as these determine, to a great extent, the character of his thought.

It is easy to declare that evil originates in the thoughts of man, that the origin of sin is in "the imaginations of the thoughts of his heart." But a rational adjustment of all things demands recognition of the fact that soundness of body is necessary to soundness of mind, that it is well-nigh impossible for an individual to be actuated by lofty aspirations and hopeful views when his physical being is disturbed by poisonous accretions or famished for vitalizing elements. It is necessary to remove the secondary cause as well as the primary. Removing the secondary, and making physical conditions as nearly perfect as is possible, makes removal of the primary cause comparatively an easy matter. That mental and physical must work together, that mind and body are supplementary agencies in establishing health and efficiency, that God and Nature are inseparable- this the Illuminati hold as fundamental truths; and on it as a foundation they are willing to stand or to fall.

Is there basis for this doctrine in revealed religion, in the Sacred Scriptures?

There is. Listen to these words, which come in thundering tones down the ages:

"What satisfieth thy mouth with good things, so that thy youth is renewed like the eagles."

How many of the vast multitudes that have read these words ever gave a thought to their meaning?

Yet how significant! How thoroughly in harmony with the doctrine of Life and Immortality! How thoroughly in harmony with the Illuminati doctrine, that "filling the mouth with good things" is a requisite of the Immortality whose "youth is renewed like the eagles!"

Let us hope that this important passage in the Scriptures may be more than a dead letter to those who read it in the light of Illuminati principles. Let us hope that humankind may hasten to accept the truth in its simplicity. Let no mystic or metaphysician regard it a materialistic doctrine which advocates that the youth of him whose mouth the Lord filleth with good things- natural, nutritious foods- is renewed like the eagles.

"Bless the Lord, O my soul; and all that is within me, bless his holy name." Bless the Lord, O my soul, and forget not all his benefits; who forgiveth all thine iniquities; who healeth all thy diseases; who redeemeth thy life from destruction; who crowneth thee with loving kindness and tender mercies; who satisfieth thy mouth with good things, so that thy youth is renewed like the eagles." Ps. 103:1-5.

These verses, in exalted poetical expression, voice the doctrine of Life and Immortality. They honor God as the Giver of all good things. They honor man as the recipient of all good things, or as the medium through which the Infinite functions. These words portray a well-balanced philosophy, a philosophy that represents God and man as counterparts, each of the other; God and Nature as harmonious co-workers; a philosophy that recognizes physical means and physical agencies as thoroughly consistent with spiritual laws and spiritual graces.

## THE TEACHING OF EUGENICS

## THE STAND TAKEN BY THE ILLUMINATI

The question of eugenics and sex hygiene is claiming pronounced attention among people generally, especially among educators and reformers. It therefore seems advisable for the Illuminati to make definite statements concerning their position on the subject.

Many have gone to great extremes in their ideas concerning eugenics and the teaching of eugenics. A few years ago it was a crime to have anything to say concerning sex and the part that sex plays in the life of man. To such extent was this the case that some who dared to speak the truth on this subject were sent to the penitentiary. Now, the pendulum of public interest has swung to the other extreme; and magazines and newspapers are full of articles on different phases of this subject as well as reports of conventions in which this subjects claims a prominent place. Indeed, to such extent is the discussion of this subject carried that the young, knowing nothing of sex, are led into all kinds of morbid conjecture.

The Illuminati hold, as they have held for many centuries, that sex is of the utmost significance, that the effects of sex, or the use of sex power, is of paramount importance. Further, they hold, as they have held in centuries past, that mankind should be taught fully concerning sex, that man should be ignorant concerning nothing that has to do with sex.

But, further than this, in the main, the Illuminati do not agree with the alarmists of the present day. The experience of those who are strenuously advocating the teaching of sex hygiene covers at best but a few years. Whereas, the experience of the Illuminati dates back through centuries. For centuries the teachers of the Illuminati have been giving instructions to their followers concerning the mysteries of sex. Proof of this fact is to be found in their literature. Their teaching has been condemned. Their teachers and writers have been persecuted because they dared to teach the truth. Nevertheless, thousands who came to the Illuminati for instruction and advice have been saved from ignorance, error, and sin. During the centuries, thousands have reaped blessings untold by following the principles of sex hygiene as advocated by the Illuminati.

And now, after many of that noble band have been made to suffer for teaching privately and quietly, under the most sacred and protected conditions, the laws of sexual science, advocates of sex hygiene are springing up on every hand, making public and prominent their plea for instruction on sex purity. To make the matter more deplorable, these would-be educators and reformers have given the science of sex little careful study. They have no practical knowledge of the principles involved. Nor do they have the slightest insight into the deeper phases of sex philosophy and its bearing on the higher culture of the human race. Nevertheless, they are bold in advocating measures which men of the Illuminati, after a lifetime of experience, would not dream of advocating. To make the contrast greater, the Illuminati teachers of past years, who reaped persecution, gave their lifetime to the study of this subject in all its phases. Their investigations resulted in the discovery of a mighty secret, which they hinted at and offered to explain to all worthy seekers after truth. But public opinion was not then ready to listen even to the barest suggestion along this line of thought. But now, under a sudden glow of enthusiasm, men of inexperience are advocating methods and systems which would result in ruin a thousand times greater than that which followed centuries of ignorance.

While the Illuminati hold, and always have held, that instruction should be given in eugenics and sexual hygiene, and that such instruction is of the utmost importance, and that upon purity of sex rests the foundation of existence, yet they emphatically condemn, not only as useless but even as a menace to humanity, the teaching of sexual hygiene in the public schools. Public opinion must be educated, to be sure. The race consciousness must be cleansed of its abnormal, morbid, and unhealthful ideas and conjectures. The race conscience must be stimulated to higher ideals and purer motives. There is urgent need of correct instruction. Knowledge, not ignorance, sets men free. Thus far the Illuminati agree with the advocates of sexual hygiene. But that the public school is the place for instruction in sexual laws is a measure which the Illuminati positively discourage. Educators in eugenics and sexual hygiene should be men and women who are qualified by nature and by careful training for imparting instruction in this especial subject. Parents are the ones in particular to whom such instruction should be given. The father should understand his own creative system, the laws of use and non-use of creative power. He should understand what subjects are wholesome to teach his sons and at what age they should be taught. The mother, likewise, should understand those things which concern her creative being and her creative power. She should know when and how to communicate true knowledge and ideas of purity and nobility to her daughters.

That children and young people as well as parents should receive instruction- in this, too, the Illuminati agree with the advocates of sexual hygiene. But that this instruction should be imparted in schools and colleges, in this, the Illuminati unreservedly disagree. No man teacher is competent to teach these subjects to boys and girls under conditions which classroom and lecture-hall make necessary. Nor is there a young woman teacher competent to handle this subject before boys of tender years, much less, boys at the age of adolescence. These statements may seem at first thought to be radical and extreme beyond reason. But careful consideration of the conditions under which teachers must work will convince any candid investigator of the truth and the wisdom of these assertions.

# THE WAY TO LIFE AND IMMORTALITY

The instructions given to parents and those who fill the place of parents should in particular emphasize the necessity of imparting wholesome information to the children under their care. In this way, rather than in the classroom, children should receive the instruction necessary to make them noble men and women. Faddists on sexual education will answer this argument by saying that the parents do not have the necessary knowledge and training themselves, and are therefore not qualified to do this. It is freely admitted that the majority are not qualified to do this as they should. But how superior is the qualification of the majority of teachers in the public schools?

Again it is fully recognized by the Illuminati that education of public opinion in this line as in all other lines is a question of time, and that conspicuous results are not to be expected on short notice. Growth and change in the race thought is at best slow. Transformation of character lies at the basis of growth. One necessary feature in the transformation of character is a practical application of the laws of eugenics and sexual power, extending through successive generations. Parents must understand hygiene and psychological laws which will enable them to procreate better and nobler specimens of humanity, children strong in body, mind, and soul. Each generation should be superior to the preceding. Thus, changes and improvements come about gradually, perhaps almost imperceptibly, nevertheless surely.

What is to be said concerning laws to regulate these matters?

The Illuminati maintain that legislative acts will confer no benefit on the race. No matter whether the laws have to do with compulsory education in the schoolroom on the science of sex or whether they aim at the regulation of marriages, little or no advantage is to be expected from them. The reasons for this conclusion are of the best. Nobility and health of offspring are to be accounted for on the basis of love and harmony between the parents and a genuine love for the child that is to be. This, no legislative measure can determine or insure. It is a fact well known to those who have given serious study to conditions which tend to better the race that it is not always the physically perfect father and mother which rear superior children, children strong in body, mind, and soul. More often, children healthy in body, strong in mind, and lofty in aspiration- aye, even geniuses, men and women who accomplish- are born to parents who, though possibly physically inferior, possess lofty desires, clean minds, and most of all, love for the forthcoming offspring. Men and women of the so-called "upper classes," although seemingly healthy in body, but desiring no children, and being in a bitter state of mind, even in a continued state of condemnation of that which is to be- these are the ones who bring forth children inferior in body and mind, and almost bereft of soul.

Through long experience, the Illuminati have observed that the father and the mother who care for each other and who desire offspring and look forward to the event with pleasure, bring forth children healthy in body and in mind, children whose souls are not warped by bitterness- and that too even though the parents may be impaired in physical health. Patent to all who have given the subject careful investigation is this observation, that even where both parents are seemingly in perfect mental and physical health, if offspring is undesired, the child will be inferior in every respect, possibly even a degenerate.

What, then, is the secret of bringing forth a race that is healthy in mind, body, and soul?

The Illuminati hold, and without successful contradiction, that, in order to accomplish this much desired object, it is necessary for parents in all walks of life, the low-born as well as the high-born, to receive instruction in regard to all phases of self-improvement and race-improvement. Race-improvement comes from improvement of individual conditions. Laws of health and hygiene must receive general attention. Parents must acquaint themselves with food values and food combinations. They must select and combine foods from the standpoint of their nourishing, and eliminating properties rather than from the standpoint of taste alone. Exercise, sleep, outdoor recreation, baths for cleanliness and for rejuvenation, proper clothing, wholesome thought environments- these and other factors which pertain to self-improvement must receive their due share of attention. People generally must become informed in regard to matters of health in body and in mind. A true system of sexual hygiene must be adopted and applied. Parents must give thoughtful consideration to the duty of instructing their children at the proper age in the science of sex. But, first and last, most important of all, it must become a part of the race consciousness to realize that there can be no healthy offspring where no offspring is desired.

The Illuminati hold it as a general principle- a principle that cannot be controverted- that one absolutely essential requisite to the birth of healthy, noble children is love and harmony between the parents. Yet, important as this factor is, it is not to be thought of as the only requisite for promoting the welfare of the race. Economic conditions must undergo renovation before we can expect normal, healthful birth and rearing of children. By no means is it true that the greatest menace to human- kind at the present time is ignorance of sexual hygiene and eugenics. The greatest menace to society, and one which is the hardest to overcome, is that state of affairs in the economic world which makes it impossible for parents to provide proper nourishment for themselves and children. Insufficient food and improper food are fundamentally accountable for disease and unhappiness and crime among the masses where ignorance of sexual hygiene is only a secondary cause. In many cases, abnormal and vicious physical appetite is directly traceable to a deranged condition of the stomach or a congested feverish slate of certain organs- all due to insufficiency of vital food elements or improper balance of food values.

# THE WAY TO LIFE AND IMMORTALITY

By no means rash and unreasonable is it to claim that the social problem and the labor question are inseparable from each other and that instruction in eugenics and sexual science will avail little unless it is supplemented by improved conditions in the industrial world, which will enable parents to provide the necessities of life for their families.

How can healthy, vigorous children be expected when the mother, during the time in which she should be provided with the best, is limited to a scanty supply of inferior food and clothing? The Illuminati therefore maintain that legal enactments regulating marriages and compelling public schools to give instruction in sexual hygiene and eugenics will be of little avail. You may make laws by the scores regulating marriages, you may compel the teachers in all schools to teach eugenics and sexual hygiene, you may even teach fathers and mothers what to do and what not to do; but, if the economic conditions are such that millions of fathers and mothers are starving while they are rearing a family, you will have deficient children, who in turn are forced to bring forth children even more deficient.

In consideration of these cold facts, facts everywhere staring us in the face, the Illuminati regard it as mockery before God and man for the church, the ministry, and well-meaning though unreasonable bodies of men and women to clamor for laws regulating marriage and laws forcing public instruction on sexual hygiene and eugenics. They know not what their feverish clamor is doing. They are advocating laws which tend to drive boys and girls to extreme measures in satisfying curiosity and conjecture unnecessarily aroused by the inadequate instruction received, even causing them to become fathers and mothers of illegitimate children. And all the while nothing is being done to control or to improve economic conditions, and the millions go on bearing children, and even the mother has not food and clothing sufficient for one body, much less for two bodies.

# THE WAY TO LIFE AND IMMORTALITY

The Illuminati admit that there is grave need of correct knowledge regarding sex. This fact can not receive too much emphasis. They admit that thousands are ruined through ignorance of this subject. But they also recognize that millions are weaklings and mental imbeciles and nervous wrecks on account of actual starvation, starvation brought about through insufficient compensation for work.

If man were simply an animal, then laws might be made forcing him not to mate unless he is in a healthy physical condition, and when himself strong and healthy to mate only with one equally strong and vigorous. Laws might then be made to appoint a guardian over him, to force him to follow the dictates of the law in all respects. In this case, he might be led to breed healthy human animals. But, even then, in order to accomplish their object, these law-makers would be compelled to provide proper food, clothing, shelter, air, sunshine, and other necessary hygienic conditions. Such items as these receive careful attention on the part of scientific breeders of animals. Admittedly, law-makers are not in a position to do this in regard to the human species, even if they have the discrimination to see that it is necessary or advisable to do so.

Man, however, is not a mere animal, nor do the laws that control animal life bind him. In procreation, man uses something more than the body. He uses mind and heart. And, under normal conditions, if the mind is in the right attitude, if the desires of both heart and mind of both father and mother are what they should be, then they will bring forth offspring which will astonish the advocates of eugenics, even though the body may be impaired in health and strength. It is love between man and woman that is the magic key to offspring which shall be efficient, of lofty spirituality, and free from disease.

For this reason, the Church of Illumination takes the stand that laws regulating marriage are useless, aye even productive of the very conditions they are trying to avoid. It holds this position in spite of all that is being said to the contrary by various churches and organizations and educators.

Before there can be a perfect human race mankind must be taught the value of hygienic conditions in all departments of life. Correct habits in regard to food, clothing, work, exercise, rest, recreation, sleep, cleanliness of both body and mind, must be generally established among men. There must be a general understanding among parents of the laws that pertain to the sexual system; and they in turn must impart such knowledge to their children. Most of all, economic conditions must be so arranged that it will be impossible for millions of deficient children to be born in the poorer sections of our cities and other places throughout the world because of an insufficiency of food to keep body and soul together.

What does the Church of Illumination propose to do as its part in the work of human redemption?

It proposes to continue teaching mankind the Divine Laws, which pertain to his entire being, which pertain to his relations with other human beings, whether it be as husband and father in the home or as worker in the employ of others or as one who gives employment to others. It proposes in its teachings to lay stress on the equal importance of man's threefold nature, physical, mental, and spiritual. It proposes to continue teaching that a sound mind and a sound body are necessary to each other; that hygienic conditions on the physical plane are equally important with psychological conditions on the mental plane; that sexual hygiene is an essential, but that it is not the only essential, to race improvement. It proposes to give a well-rounded, well-balanced education and training to those who seek solace and help within its temple doors. It proposes to guard against abnormal emphasis on any one department of life.

THE WAY TO LIFE AND IMMORTALITY

Furthermore, the instruction offered by the Illuminati on the subject of sex is not experimental. It is not the work of well-meaning, though abnormally enthusiastic, amateurs. It is the result of life-long investigations, the result of successful experience through centuries of time. The instructions have been tested under varied conditions in different climes and in different periods of history- all with satisfactory results to those who have obeyed the laws in their manifold requirements. The Illuminati are prepared to give scientific instruction on the varied aspects of this subject, including sexual hygiene, eugenics, duty of parents to each other, and duly of parents to their offspring. But, most important of all, they are prepared to teach both to the married and to the unmarried the sacredness of sex, and the power of sex in unfolding the Divine Image in man and woman. There is power in sex undreamed of by the most radical advocate of eugenics- power which concerns not only the physical man but the spiritual man as well, power which directly and undeniably affects the soul, power which, when properly directed, becomes the Way to Life and Immortality. The higher features of sexual science, the features that pertain to soul culture, immortality, and rejuvenation of the entire being, are items of which the multitudes little dream. But these deeper truths are the very things which the Illuminati have been teaching, are teaching, and propose to continue teaching mankind.

Moreover, the minister, or the priest, of the Illuminati may not, dare not, officiate in marrying a man and a woman who have not received instruction in the various departments of sexual science. These instructions are in the form of lessons covering no less than forty-eight hours all told. They contain the fundamental laws which concern the betterment of the race. They are prepared specifically for those who contemplate marriage, and are given privately to the prospective husband and wife prior to the marriage ceremony. Thus, it is evident that the Temple of Illuminati is far in advance of other organizations which aim at race betterment. None can belong to it and be in ignorance of the Foundation of Life.

# THE WAY TO LIFE AND IMMORTALITY

## THE WAY TO GODHOOD

### BE THOU A MAN AND THOU MAYST BE A GOD

We have stepped from the old life with its teaching's, its religions, its philosophies, which have taught men a negative and destructive doctrine and thereby have held them in bondage and in slavery for many centuries, with its teachings of the undesirableness of life, the evil of worldly possessions, the destructive effects of natural desires and passions, the evils of joy and happiness on earth. We have left these things behind, and have stepped into the new age, wherein we are taught that manhood is the way to Godhood, that life is glorious and desirable, that happiness and joy is the divine heritage of man, and that all men have the right to develop power and strength so that they may be a success, so that they may have possessions which will give them strength and power, influence and desirable things in life, without robbing others of these same desirable things.

### BE A MAN AND THOU MAYST BE A GOD

This is the Divine Command of the New Age. Because this one new command includes the Ten Commandments given by the Lawgiver Moses and even more than these, it is to be regarded more important than the Decalogue. The new book of which this command is the theme teaches the new religion-science-philosophy, teaches man how to be a man, teaches him how to live so that he may have health, strength, and power, so that he may possess those things which bring happiness and peace, teaches him the right and the desirability of living. The book teaches him that happiness on earth is the path to happiness in the next world; for no man can be truly happy who is living an evil life.

**THE END**